After Barnardo

Ann Howard
Eric Leonard

*The phenomenon of child migration
from Tilbury to Sydney from 1921-1965*

As a contented family man, I applaud members of the largest family in the world whose lives are described in After Barnardo. Their successes are hard won and they should be doubly applauded.

Mark Taylor
former Captain of the Australian Cricket Team
Australian of the Year 1999

TARKA Publishing 1999

Acknowledgements

My gratitude to Rod Atfield, Managing Director of Mercantile Mutual whose generous sponsorship made this book possible and who gave a free hand to my authorship.

Thank you to Eric Leonard for approaching Rod Atfield and helping to realise what had long been the aim of the Barnardo Old Boys and Girls in having their stories recorded. Thank you for the support, encouragement, trust and patience of child migrants, their families and friends.

The photographs came from many sources, including the Musee de Ville, Noumea and are most gratefully acknowledged.

Thank you in alphabetical order, to:
The Australian Society of Archivists, Barnardos Australia, Robert Bickerstaff, Collette Bradford, Lyndall Eeg, the Fairbridge Foundation, Bill Hoyles, Bev Kingston, Neil Morrison, Bill Moverley, the National Archives of Australia, the National Library of Australia, Doreen Norman, Geoff Pritchard, Shirley Ronge, The Royal Australian Historical Society, Margaret Schmitt, the Society of Australian Genealogists, the State Library of New South Wales and Harbour Master Tom Strasser.

Thank you for the unfailing generosity of experts in different fields, some of whom requested to remain anonymous.

Ann Howard MA M Sci Soc

Other books by Ann Howard

Australia and World War I
Roads and Highways
Coaches, Riverboats and Railways
Cattle Drovers
Australia and World War II
From Colonies to Commonwealth
Women in Australia
You'll Be Sorry!
Where Do We Go From Here?
A Century of Life

Under preparation: -
Juvenile Sea Diaries
The Meaning of Home

Cover photo: In May 1998, Eric Leonard was revisiting Boy's Garden City, Woodford Bridge, Essex, which by then was being partly demolished to make way for the Prince Regent Hotel. While clambering over the rubble, he found a photo of his little mate, Ken Church, from the 1930's, eating peas pudding and polony. He rescued the photo and it became the cover for *After Barnardo 1*. Ken, who became a millionaire tells his story on page 76.

National Library of Australia Cataloguing-in-Publication
©Howard, Ann 1942-
After Barnardo 1

Bibliography
ISBN 0-646-35113-3

1. British/Australian Child Migrants 2. Barnardo Migrants
3. Child Migrants 1921-1965 4. Child Labour I. Title

TARKA Publishing
Dangar Island 2083

©Howard, Ann 1999.
After Barnardo 1
ISBN 0-646-35113-3
All rights reserved
Printed and bound in Australia

Production notes: written and designed by Ann Howard from TARKA.
Designed with QuarkXPress 4.04 and Adobe Photoshop 5.0 on Mac.
Printed by Agency Press.

 haracter is better than ancestry and personal conduct of more importance than the highest parentage...

Dr Thomas John Barnardo

Dedication
This book is dedicated to child migrants through time

After Barnardo 1 draws on original material from child migrants who have felt able to speak to Ann, many for the first time, about being sent from Dr Barnardo's Homes in the UK to Sydney, in ships and later by plane, from 1921 to 1965, as a result of adult decision making. Without choice, they were described as 'voluntary'. About 150 000 migrant children were sent from British orphanages, homes and charitable organisations to Canada, Australia, Bermuda, New Zealand, South Africa, Zimbabwe and the Caribbean from 1869 to1965.

*S*ometimes harrowing, often moving, the stories in *After Barnardo*, of success as well as failure in the face of adversity, illustrate the triumph of the human spirit.

Eric Leonard is one of these success stories. He arrived in Sydney in 1937, in the *Otranto*, a smiling Barnardo's boy. After working as a jackaroo, cane cutter, wool classer and NSW mounted policeman, he joined us as an agent in 1980, and has performed a very valuable service to his clients and to Mercantile Mutual ever since.

Eric met Ann Howard, when she was writing *A Century of Life* for our centenary and they have collaborated in the production of this extraordinary book.

Part of 100 years of the history of our great company has been the support of many worthwhile causes. Records show donations from the staff at Mercantile Mutual to Dr Barnardos as early as 1939, with yearly donations since.

Mercantile Mutual has been pleased to make available for posterity these accounts from the lips of those sent unwittingly as children from Tilbury Docks to Sydney from 1921 to 1965 recorded by Ann.

Rod Atfield
Managing Director
Mercantile Mutual

August 1999

CONTENTS

FORM OF REGISTRATION FOR TOWN LADS

(AS USED THROUGHOUT THIS MOVEMENT).

IMPERIAL MIGRATION FOR LADS.

**Read the Notice on the back of this paper, and if you want to go
Farming in the Colonies fill up the Form below.**

Name (in full)_____

Address_____

_____

Height_____feet_____inches.   Weight_____stone_____lbs.

Age_____   Date of birth_____191   .

Nature of all employ- ⎰ _____
ment since leaving   ⎱ _____
School   _____
                          _____

Are you now in work?_____   Present or last wages?_____

Present (or last) Employer_____

_____

Have you your Parents' consent?_____

Have you had any agricultural experience?_____
(State whether you can milk, drive, ride, or plough.)

What religious persuasion do you belong to?_____
(*e.g.*, Church of England, Roman Catholic, Wesleyan, &c.)

Trade or occupation of Father_____

Names and Addresses ⎰ _____
of people to whom   ⎱ _____
application must be   _____
made for references

(Original references should not be sent until asked for.)

Can you provide your own outfit?_____   (*See Note* 10 *on next page.*)

Can you pay a deposit of £3 on your fare?_____
(Those paying £3 themselves will be sent first.)

Which Colonies would you prefer?_____
(*See Note* 11 *on next page.*)

Do you agree with the terms on the back of this Form?_____

*Date*_____191   .   (*Signature*)_____

This form, when filled up and signed, to be returned to Mr.

Wilful misstatements in filling up this Form will be regarded as attempted fraud.

ISSUED BY THE LORDS
COMMISSIONERS OF HIS
MAJESTY'S TREASURY
UNDER THE AUTHORITY

*M*en and women walk Australian streets who will never know their true names or ages. Deported from the UK as children, sometimes without parental consent, many never retained contact with any of their relatives. They matured, married, pursued careers and achieved success, often living with a general chronic melancholy, refusing to be vulnerable, internalising feelings. With distant memories always pursued, forgetting is as important as remembering as they are forced to make a life narrative from fragments. Some still search.

*M*any questions remain
Why was it an option: who were these children: why so many: why were they sent to Australia: why lied to: why did Australia demand more: why were only the brightest and best sent: why were many only allowed on the land or in domestic service: why were they separated from brothers and sisters and loved foster parents: why were their records withheld: why did they often have to bear the humiliation of the unloved: why were lines of communication broken between them and their kin? With the grim wisdom of hindsight we glimpse into the lives that these migrants led to gain insight into the complicated truth.

When Myfanwy Shapland finally got her papers, there was a strange little handwritten unsigned note among them which read, 'Mother very attached but not well off or very robust. Why was she sent to Australia?' Most were relinquished or abandoned by relatives when little, but many wrongly believed themselves orphans. For sixty years, Peter Chaffey believed his brother, Reginald had died on the ship to Australia, until he contacted the Child Migrant Trust. Reginald Chaffey migrated in 1937, but his sick brother, Peter stayed in Boys Garden City, UK. Reginald was happy at Mowbray Park, Australia but

Eva Unwin, (right), and Violet Knight at their foster home, 'Great Rollright' Oxfordshire. Vi remembers the thatched cottage and the plum tree behind them. She says: I loved Eva, she was my family. I came to Australia because of her

1

one day in 1938 became ill. The boys were looking forward to the Picton Show and so he kept quiet. At the show, the little snowy haired, fair skinned boy collapsed and was taken to Camden Hospital, with diphtheria, where he died shortly afterwards. Eric Leonard was able to place flowers on Reginald's grave in Australia for Peter. Through the Trust, Peter later found two half brothers in Kent.

No migrant from the earlier period had migration explained to them. Even if authorities or relations acted for the best, they later felt betrayed. The overwhelming power of authority kept everyone unquestioning.

Henry Wheeler remembers: It wasn't until papers and records were open to us that I realized that I must have family. I received papers from After Care in Sydney in 1983. My admittance card showed my grandfather and mother lived in Deddington and I took it on myself to write to the Deddington address knowing that it was a very long shot because the address was from 1927. To my shock and amazement, I received a letter from the local printer, that his father knew the Wheeler family who used to live there and that I had a brother living in Kenilworth and that my mother was still alive. He forwarded the address of my brother. We immediately got in contact, missing meeting my mother by three months.

Family members often falsely believed each other dead for years. Victims rescued by Barnardo's and rehabilitated were shipped out to become victims again, trapped in an emotional vacuum of unrelenting domestic work or on country properties until 21 years old. Some suspect or know for certain that they have not inherited property in the UK which is lawfully theirs. On admittance to Barnardo's, these children became part of the largest family in the world. Sometimes this remained their only family. They have a special rapport with each other. Shirley Ronge, whose mother committed suicide shortly after they were reunited, knows how many feel, as she has walked a hard path, and she visits many older migrants, to sit and talk with them as only a fellow migrant can.

Some children were glad to escape the conditions they endured, especially in the Depression. Fred Dyke, who migrated in 1925, remembers: While I was a lad in the Portsmouth workhouse, an older man used to tell me what a great place Australia was. At Barnardo's, the magistrate asked me if I'd like to emigrate, I said I would, and that I wanted to be a boundary rider.

Contributors to this book are now able to share their experiences with us. Understandably, many others cannot. Some children and parents have committed suicide: the distress level being unbearable. A few withdrew their contribution because of pressure from relatives or feelings of loyalty to their employer's children. Some child migrants, like Dermott Reilly, were able to adjust to their situation and make a success of their lives in every way. Thelma Pold (Reeves), who migrated in 1939, was encouraged by Miss Dobbie, and Miss Bocking, her Headmistress and staff, to become a teacher, the career she followed until she was 53 years old. Some, like Eric Leonard, were able to help other emotionally distraught people.

Some migrants were treated as family members, but some were abused and degraded. Some ran away, one stayed with her family for 74 years. Some, like Roger Slaughter, married and settled happily in the area where they were first placed.

2

Conditions for child migrant workers in early days involved eating separately from their employers, sleeping outside in rough housing like animals, and working from 4am to 10pm, on such low wages that they could not freely go. Some had half a day off each week, but had to finish their work first. Some had to address the employer's sons as 'master'.

James Hill remembers: On my seventeenth birthday I was sent to a 27 000 acre Hunter Valley property. The owners were from the old British style of aristocracy. I lived in an old unlined tin hut, with two round saplings cut from the bush, nailed to the wall and covered with chaff bags, with a chaff bag stuffed with straw for a mattress. I had my meals, mostly bread and mutton, in the laundry among the dirty washing. I had to wash in the creek and there was no furniture in my quarters.(1924)

Bill Moverley says: I was ten when I arrived in the *Barrabool*. When I went on the land after Mowbray Park farm school, at fourteen, we were treated like chattels. One Sunday, I took the pony over the paddocks to the next property to see young John Buxton. He was sitting alone with his head in his hands. He told me that the boss was working him to death, eighteen hour days. I knocked on the boss's door and asked him why. 'Are you a Communist?' he asked. One boss only banked two shillings a week for me, which I didn't find out for a long time and one boss was so disagreeable that I shot a bucket of milk over him and walked off without even changing my clothes. I thought I'd go fruit picking in the next state, but the police brought you back. (1934)

Barnardo boys not slave labour (*Sunday Telegraph headline, November 29th, 1921)*
One arresting question that arises from the testimony of child migrants from the twenties to the forties is, were they slaves? Some participants stated vehemently that they were and that a class of child slaves was created in Australia.

Anonymous: I came out to Ashfield on December 3rd 1936. On the 8th, five or six of us were put on a train to Canberra, like sheep, you just went. I was picked up and taken to a grazier's property miles from anywhere. The cook left, then the children's nurse left, and I was left with everything. They had two children aged four and six. I grew quite fond of them, but I never had a day off unless she took the children to a birthday party and then I went with them. I had to put wet newspaper on the floor then sweep it with a millet broom, clean the silver tureens, wash the clothes in a copper and iron with a flat iron off the stove. I served at table and always ate in the kitchen. I had seven shillings and sixpence a week, with five shillings banked by Barnardo's and two shillings to pay off my uniform. My afternoon dress was yellow, crossed over and tied at the side, with a frilly muslin apron. I wore a hat tied at the back with ribbons. Miss Wedlock came to inspect the situation every six months.

3

Assigned convicts and child migrant workers

The convicts represented all levels of society, child migrants were picked from the brightest and best, but the labour of both was useful. After 1833, assigned convicts worked from sunrise to sunset with an hour for breakfast and lunch, a half day Saturday and Sunday free. Some child migrants quoted far longer hours. Henry Wheeler remembers: Aged fourteen, I was given all the hardest tasks and worked 16 hours a day, seven days a week.(1930) Severe physical punishment meted out to assigned convicts could result in instant or delayed death, but child migrants could be beaten with sticks or abused. Assigned convicts had redress to the bench, although they might not get justice, magistrates usually being powerful landholders with mutual interests. Protests continued in spite of failure and drastic punishment. 'Tis in their blood to expect fairness', one observer wrote of English labourers. The *NSW Juvenile Migrants' Apprentice Act of 1924*, required guardianship for juvenile migrants until aged 21. Migrant child workers were checked by Barnardo's inspectors, but they gave advance notice of visits, so conditions would temporarily improve, and the young worker was disempowered by being interviewed in front of their employer. Times were hard, as employment was scarce. Young workers were encouraged to stay because it was some kind of job. They were also taught to be grateful. The community they had been drawn from was imbued with these attitudes. Nobody asked questions. Ken Church says: My foster father looked up from the fields and waved goodbye as I was whisked away in a car, never to see him again.(1937)

Indigenous people were lower. An anonymous participant remembers: I was working from dawn to dusk on a farm miles from anywhere. On my half day off there was no-where to go so I wrote letters or sat around. Once, an aboriginal girl from the next farm went with me to the pictures. She was very nice. I was only allowed to do this once, because when my employer's wife found out she didn't approve.(1936)

Home in time for tea?

A child migrant - is this the appropriate term? Asked if they would like to go with an Australian party, meaning migration, many children thought it was for a birthday. Tom Price, MBE, Senior Lieutenant Royal Navy retired and beloved 'pop' to many Barnardo children, recounted a five year old 'voluntary migrant' tugging at his trouser leg on board, asking 'Will I be home in time for tea?'. Free will is implied in the word ' migration', as 'to move from one place to settle in another', not the nightmare of losing family and country.

Migration is by compulsion or attraction. Migrants flee from religious persecution, justice, war, poverty, racial discrimination or perceived lack of opportunity. They may join relatives, buy cheap land or take up government incentives. Always an enormous undertaking, migration can result in a lifelong positive outcome of peace and prosperity, which, fortunately, it did in the long term for many child migrants.

Harry Gerstle, a Townsville resident was German born. He was awarded the Order of Australia in 1985, particularly for work with the Royal Queensland Bush Children's Health Scheme. He says: Things did not look too rosy for people of a non-Aryan background. An invitation from an Australian relative was accepted with alacrity. I was 15, too young to travel alone, so my parents, learning that a group of Barnardo boys would be travelling in the *Otranto*, asked if the leaders would keep a watchful eye on me.(1937)

This child migrant phenomenon is not an isolated incident and happens today, in many cases saving lives, for instance in Roumania. The alternative to child migration could be death, disease, or lifelong poverty, mostly through lack of paid work for any members of their family group.

May Chandler says: I was a sickly child - I had complications after a tonsillectomy. I was seven when I went into the Homes and I don't remember anything before that. Mother couldn't keep us, we were neglected and my father was never on the scene. There were five of us... they asked at school 'Who would like to go to Australia?' All the kids said 'Yes!' I was nine when I came out and it didn't dawn on me what was really involved as we were a big party on the boat and very well looked after. Miss Shauvess looked after us at Sweetbriar Cottage before we came out helped us to get to know each other. She came out with us. I named my first house Sweetbriars. I went to Ashfield. Madge and I with Arthur Hook were in a photo running up a slope which was used as a Barnardo's tram advertisement. I loved Picton very much. I wrote away for my history to England but it had deteriorated so badly, I could hardly read the photo copy. I tried to save up and see my mother - she died in 1972.(1937)

Severing all ties

Why was migration an option? It seems extraordinary, to officially sanction the deportation of children, some as young as six, over 13 000 miles away often severing all ties from their relatives, who by the nature of things should have their best interests at heart.

5

Long before being considered by Dr Barnardo, migration was an expedient measure. In 1618, a group of destitute English children arrived in Richmond, Virginia. In 1629 the first Governor of Boston remarked in his *Reasons for Emigration*, 'England contained too many people and competition there was too keen'. 1790 saw the emigration of 500 of the 1900 inhabitants of just one Scottish town to help establish Long Island, USA, after traditional farming was replaced by commercial sheep farming. Many who would never have dreamed of emigrating were compelled to take the expensive and dangerous step. People emigrate now, both legally and illegally, and in the future will emigrate to other planets.

Valerie Peccard, seated on the left with her descendants, was one of ten orphan girls sent to Noumea in the Empress Eugenie. *The following year, thirty more were sent. Between 1871 and 1880, 4 250 French citizens were deported to New Caledonia*

God prosper the people who sent us away.

Convicts, whether adults or children, were not encouraged to look on deportation as a welcome move, although many prospered. Henry and Samuel O-, in a statement to Commissioner Bigge: Arrived in 1836. Am now on a piece of land, 20 acres; myself and brother Samuel, live together; both are single; we make a good living...I have never heard from my friends...left a mother at home...I was very young when sent here; hardly knew good from bad, my brother was 11, I was 12. Bigge advocated the employment of convicts as shepherds to protect them against the immorality of towns, in true Victorian vein.

Australia, first unfashionable as a destination, became seen as an open door to opportunity. Just two popular migrant characters who made their fortunes by the time Thomas Barnardo was born in Dublin were Dicken's Mr Micawber (Micawber, have you ever considered emigration?...Say to Australia?...Perhaps on that distant shore something good will turn up), and Estelle's convict father in *Great Expectations. Punch* printed a cartoon captioned '*1848. Here and there, or Emigration a Remedy*', showing first a homeless family in the streets, then well-fed and dressed, with hams hanging from the ceiling, in their comfortable colonial home. Emigration was related to poverty, as by the stinging Wakefieldian phrase of 'shovelling out paupers'. Shipping groups of children from their overcrowded homeland was officially sanctioned in 1850. Under the *Poor Law Amendment Act,* Boards of Guardians could send children under sixteen from workhouses to Canada.

To seek for employment
Where work can be found
To meet with enjoyment
On less crowded ground
We cross the broad ocean
With gladness and glee

And when in devotion
We're bending the knee
This, this shall our prayer be
At the close of each day
God prosper the people who
Sent us away
Ragged School Union Magazine

Dr Barnardo sent 'little rescued gutter lads' to Canada, saying 'migration confers upon the children themselves unspeakable blessings'. Thousands of children died in the teeming streets of the UK, one in five, before their fifth birthday. Children regarded as refuse became clean, smiling, well-dressed Protestant migrants, photographed, farewelled by royalty and heralded as guardians of the Empire. Was migration a solution to the seemingly unstoppable tidal wave of human degradation? Keeping a child in Britain cost £16 a year, only £10 in Canada. The party of eight boys sent to Australia in 1883, was the beginning of the wave of 2 784 child migrants described in this book.

Where did all these children come from?
The Elizabethans sent vagabond children overseas from what they considered overcrowded cities and ports, but the Victorian population boom would have stunned them. Previously, three quarters of children born are estimated to have died. All levels of society were affected, none of Queen Anne's eighteen children surviving. Children died and adult deaths continued which resulted in a slow population growth from 1801 to 1871, with an estimated population of only two million in the UK. Then, the birth rate soared dramatically while the death rate dropped, mostly because of increased medical knowledge, better nutrition and bureaucratic concern for public health.

The steep population increase and speed of change of the new experience of the Industrial Revolution, caused enormous distress. Young rural people without inheritance migrated to industrially vitalised cities, retaining only limited family ties. Dr Barnardo wrote: For many years there has been an exodus from the country to towns: girls abandon domestic service for factory life: country life is dull, it's hard to find accommodation and wages are lower... I have tried training boys for English rural life and they run away.

Workers poured into cities attracted by the industrial boom, but unemployment and epidemics fragmented families. The month that Barnardo opened his mission, cholera and smallpox were rife. The Registrar-General reported people of all ages falling ill every hour as if poisoned. An eye witness saw thirty bodies in a room with no-one to bury them. Barnardo attended as many as sixteen deaths a day. Large numbers of children were unsupported.

The same problems had been present in Australia. Anna King, wife of the Governor, was horrified on her return to Sydney in 1800 to learn of more than 1 000 street urchins stealing and prostituting themselves in the small settlement. She hastily set up the Bridge Street orphanage for girls.

In both places, children had been abandoned or driven into the streets with shouts and blows by desperate parents, the enormity of the problem neither analysed nor accepted. With burgeoning numbers of waifs, attitudes were brutalised. Mothers birthing these children were the undeserving poor, especially if they were without visible means of support.

The undeserving poor

The poor were blamed for their condition partly because of an essay by Thomas Malthus, who stated in 1798, that population always outruns production, making deep poverty, vice and misery inescapable. He retracted this in his second essay, but for the next century, his initial claims were adopted by social planners. Seeing poor relief as sheer folly, he stressed that workhouses should not be 'comfortable asylums' but places where 'fare should be hard'. The spectre of this teaching haunted all those falling haplessly into a poverty trap. William Pitt introduced a 1796 *Parliamentary Bill* for family allowances as 'a matter of right or honour', but withdrew it in the light of Malthus's dismal doctrine.

Gladys Williams, daughter of Dr Barnardo's biographer, wrote: One of my earliest recollections is visiting the Doctor's famous model village at Barkingside, Essex, in the early 1910's. I had no idea then what a pioneer venture this village had been when the Doctor first started it some forty years earlier - in days when abandoned children were herded by the hundred into barrack workhouses with adult paupers, thieves and beggars, thrust into pauper uniforms, ticketed and numbered, little girls with their heads cropped, and every atom of love, beauty, colour and tenderness drilled out of their young lives

Society's attitudes disempowered parents, especially single ones. Women, who had scant opportunity for paid work and little choice about birth, were almost entirely dependent on male breadwinners. There was no welfare net. A woman trying to keep children clean and fed, fell quickly into a poverty trap. In winter in the northern hemisphere, it is impossible to dry washing or heat rooms without money. Frozen sheets hang without drying for weeks. As family structures disintegrated, supporting parents, the young and very old were the first victims. Migrants today read painfully about the 'fallen women', 'women of bad character', 'loose morals' and 'easy virtue' that were their mothers. Admission papers as late as the 1940's demonstrate the persistent moral censure of women. Reports were only meant for the eyes of officials. It was never foreseen that one day relatives would read them through the *Freedom of Information Act.*

The emerging Victorian middle class immersed itself in conspicuous consumerism, parading elaborate bonnets, dresses, furniture and accessories, needing armies of support workers. Elaborate rituals accompanied eating, walking, where to sit, how to sit, whom to sit with, what to say and to whom. An uneasy nouveau riche comforted and reassured itself, singing round the piano, embroidering, fainting and sweeping from church to home, visiting, shopping, riding in horse drawn carriages and trains, weighed down with trappings and symbol, while the underclass swelled. Social pretensions had been transported to Australia and persisted for 100 years. In Australia, in 1839, Louisa Meredith commented sarcastically on the mismatch of highly priced horses and carriages. Pre-war child migrants placed in domestic and farmwork, found themselves eating apart from and after the employer's family, even when the homestead was a shack, a bewildered component of the status quo. Anonymous: At one place, the female cook and another single chap - I could never work out his position, lived and ate with the boss and his family at all times. I ate alone in the kitchen. My Christmas dinner was brought out after the family had been served. They sent out a bottle of beer, as a peace offering, I think.

*T*oo many children

For people scratching a subsistence in a cold climate, 'childhood' in current terminology, did not exist. Most children worked as soon as they could crawl, considered capable of a man's labour aged eleven. The capitalistic structure defined the concept of a 'child'. They had to work and now there were, 'too many children' to be part of it.

A different concept of 'child' evolved with middle class Victorian children enjoying lavish nurseries, governesses, special clothes, wonderful toys and fairy stories. Nursery rhymes mostly come from Victorian England's middle class. Dr Barnardo brought dirty, neglected children from the gutters and gave them the same appealing image.

Gladys Williams, daughter of Dr Barnardo's biographer: 'For me his village was a marvellous Never-Never Land. Clean dainty little girls with shining waist-long hair went happily about their affairs and giant rocking horses smiled out at me from playroom windows. The girls let me share their games, swings, seesaws and even took me on daring expeditions over to the brook to peer about for the water rat. What intelligent child wouldn't have wanted to be an orphan and stay there for life?'

The Barnardo children were often better off than their counterparts. Mrs Barnardo wrote: 'Amongst a people professing to follow One who said, 'Suffer the little children to come unto Me', and 'Inasmuch as ye have done it unto one of the least of these,' the children starved in the gutters and there were few to care...in the sight of the law they were the property of their parents, to be traded with, and kicked, and starved, and, short of murder, parental rights without parental responsibility, were upheld by the highest tribunals'.

One anonymous migrant, who was gently bred, had a rude awakening in Australia. She said: Mrs Turner did the washing and cleaning, and a Miss Bow took us for walks. We had 'mother' and Gladys Redford, the maid. We were fed beautifully. We went to the Co-op for groceries and the girls working there made a fuss of us and knitted us tam o' shanters. We were called 'Miss Spackman's little girls'. The local gentry invited us for special occasions. As I was put in the Homes as a little baby, I did not miss a loving home and I only remember being very happy. Arriving in Australia, I was driven out to a country property and asked to dress three freshly killed chickens. Staring at their dripping necks, I asked, 'What in?' We were expected to carry hot billies of tea and scones on horseback to the men in the fields, bending over to untie the gates, cook for ten people and work on the property. Dead snakes were draped over fences. All we knew was how to play.

Fallen women

The process of becoming a 'fallen woman' could begin with the uneasy alliance between a woman and her employer, especially in domestic service. To conceive and have no visible means of support meant the beginning of a downward spiral to prostitution and death. Young women were disempowered by ignorance of their own biological condition and lack of financial resources. They were shunned by a whispering community. It is difficult to appreciate the fear and emotion evoked by the words 'born out of wedlock', or 'illegitimate' or 'bastard' in early Victorian to postwar times throughout the English speaking world. Many relinquished children were illegitimate.

Mary Allison says: My grandmother was in service and became pregnant. She got fourteen shillings and sixpence a week from the father until her daughter, my mother, was also able to go into service. My mother was a 'good girl', who was 'walking out with a young man' and living at home with my grandmother. In one week, she went into hospital, gave birth to me and died of puerperal fever. She did not know she was pregnant. Her mother didn't know she was pregnant. Her fiance was unaware of her condition. He said, very sadly, that he would have cared for the child. My grandmother cared for me for a while but was too old to cope and so I went into Barnardo's.

The children who bore the taint of illegitimacy found it affected every facet of their place in society. They suffered from feelings of discomfort at school to distress at having their passport stamped 'illegitimate', to highly charged complex emotions at presenting documents, or not having any, for a job, for medical reasons, to the bank, or in meeting prospective in-laws, or men of the cloth. Church and state joined in condemning birth outside marriage. Welfare was often withheld from single mothers on the grounds that they were immoral.

S hared attitudes

Lack of concern for women and children, transported to early nineteenth century Australia, was aggravated by pioneering conditions, as illustrated in *Fought and Won* by J Lewis, 1822: Just at daylight ...I saw an object coming towards me...I noticed she had her skirt rolled up and I heard sounds...her hair was hanging over her shoulder and she looked as if she was crying...I asked her what was making that noise and she told me she had given birth to a child that night..she was travelling with a team that was going to Johnny Downs, but that they had gone on and left her...

In 1826 Governor George Arthur, in Tasmania, ordering a survey of the poor children of Hobart Town asked for information on destitute children and was immediately presented with a list of 100 at risk. Nurseries, sometimes 'baby farms' run by single men, had a high infant mortality rate. One, in Hobart in 1833, lost 40 of the 108 admitted. In Victoria in 1891, the largest category of parents of neglected children was that of women in indigent circumstances. A report to parliament in that year, shows 238 women in this group, of which 61 were widows, 72 deserted wives, 21 had husbands in prison, 7 had husbands in lunatic asylums. Children were further at risk during the pastoral, commercial and industrial depression between 1885 and 1905, when employment became a crucial issue and it was difficult for women to find paid work. The high level of distress was shown by crowds of unemployed men marching through the streets in 1892, to form 'turbulent assemblages'.

In England, complacency in the middle classes was reinforced with self congratulation. There were attempts at 'good works', mostly from a sanctimonious distance, but no welfare net. George Bernard Shaw raged in the *London Star*, in 1888: Such is the stark-naked reality of these abominable bastard Utopias of genteel charity, in which the poor are first robbed and then pauperised by way of compensation, in order that the rich man may combine the luxury of the protected thief with the unctuous self-satisfaction of the pious philanthropist.

Women, defined as property, but unable to own any, entered the marriage market at considerable risk. The thought of 'marrying beneath one,' made mothers shudder in drawing rooms. Havelock Ellis in *Man and Woman*,1894: There is...no country in the world, certainly no civilised country, in which a woman may safely state her wishes and desires and proceed openly to their satisfaction.

Maude Torode, a 1925 migrant, was cited admiringly by A W Green to the Under Secretary of the Department of Labour and Industry in July 1930: (after domestic service) she entered the Women's Hospital for Training and passed her final exam in June 1930. She is to enter the Royal Prince Alfred Hospital for general training, when she will have her general certificate. She is a girl we all feel very proud of, as she has been faced with financial difficulties but has always upheld her dignity and independence.

The poor were romanticised in paintings with well-fed middle class children handing prettily ribboned baskets of food through locked spear-tipped iron gates to rosy-faced beggars, quite different from the reality of blue-faced mites shivering, starving and dying on cold stone steps. Homeless of all ages were herded into workhouses, where they slept on straw, barely existing. In Malthusian thinking, to encourage them to stay was to encourage indolence. Children hid from the police. Relying on the kindness of strangers, they froze to death and died of hunger, half hidden in empty crates and barrels in wet alleyways and under windswept bridges.

Phrases such as 'work is the curse of the drinking classes', helped further brutalise attitudes towards a problem that seemed to have no solution. Lord Shaftesbury observed, 'several members of the tribe, bold, pert and dirty as London sparrows, but pale, feeble and sadly inferior to them in plumpness of outline...the foul and dismal passages are thronged with children from both sexes...though wan and haggard, they are singularly vivacious...the matted hair, the disgusting filth...and the barbarian freedom from all superintendence and restraint, fills the mind...with perplexity and dismay...those that are clothed are grotesque, the tail-coats frequently trail below the heels'. An attempt to help one unfortunate was held up for public acclaim as a throng of unfortunates clamoured for help.

*A*child takes a man's hand
In Barnardo's voluntary London 'Ragged School', in a rented donkey stable in 1868, a destitute boy, Jim Jarvis, begged to sleep by the fire. Barnardo questioned him and the realisation hit him: Is it possible that in this great city there are others also homeless and destitute, who are as young as this boy, as helpless, and as ill-prepared as he to withstand the trials of cold, hunger and exposure?

Even this remarkable man, working in the East End, where hundreds of children hid at night, was not aware that a child could actually be homeless, until his hand was taken by young Jim Jarvis. He was shown semi-naked children wriggling like eels under tarpaulins in the market, and hanging over roofs to get warmth from chimney stacks. It is a paradox that he was taken by one trusting child's hand to reveal a problem so huge that it could only be tackled by institutions. The social problems were so immense that the good doctor had to take draconian measures. The problem had been allowed to escalate to an almost unsolvable level with a tide of wretchedness which initially he could not hope to alleviate only divert.

Barnardo rescued children in the face of fierce opposition. He freely admitted: I have myself frequently bought little children for a mere trifle. I have also smuggled children quietly away or I have abducted them almost by force in the face of angry opposition...the rescue of hundreds of children in the streets of London can only be accomplished in defiance of the law of the land...I am convinced I have moral law on my side.

Barnardo knew that the help he offered was not perfect. He called his homes, 'beautiful machines'. 'I have a family of 20 girls in one of the cottages...but did you ever know a family of 20 daughters?', he wrote. The responses he made were to the exigencies of the times.

Small solutions

Realising his mammoth task, Barnardo personalised poverty. Dramatising wretchedness, hunger and despair, by photographing the children one by one, firstly in their destitution and then clean, well fed and smiling, he offered small solutions to which the public, aristocracy and politicians were able to respond.

His principles were published in the Annual Report for 1889: Destitute children received without limitation as to age, sex, creed or nationality, irrespective of any kind of physical infirmity, crippled, maimed, deformed, or blind children, deaf-mutes, incurables, and even those given over to death are eligible if really destitute at any hour of the day or night, solely on their merits without election, and without the intervention of wealthy patrons. Records show that admittances were according to his principles. Children came originally from Australia, Africa, Rio de Janeiro, USA, Germany, Japan and the West Indies as well as all over the British Isles.

13

A shy man, of small stature, he wrote and spoke publicly with increasing courage, appealing for voluntary help, clothes, books, funds. People responded emotionally. In 1877, a young servant girl is said to have pressed a brown paper bag into his hands with 27 farthings in it. Barnardo, a religious man, saw this as a positive sign for his life's work.

Stepney Causeway

In 1874 the first Ever-Open-Door opened at No 10 Stepney Causeway. Nos 6 and 8 were added later. No 18 Stepney Causeway was triumphantly acquired in 1870: 'The house was old and tumbledown, every floor of which shook under a heavy tread, in a narrow and squalid street hard by Stepney Station on the Commercial Road', wrote Dr Barnardo. No 18 overflowed into No 20 then 22 and then Nos 18-26.

Careful documentations of every case brought under public scrutiny by Barnardo, appalled and fascinated the Victorian mind. He describes in *Night and Day* January to February 1880, an Irish baby, mother dead in childbirth, father a drunkard, with a face 'like that of a little old woman, sitting on the ground and sucking a piece of candle with its hard gums'.

A West Indian widow, whose loved husband, a freed man, died saving a drowning comrade, kept her three children warm in sacks which she sewed for one penny. A kindly landlady and some neighbours tried to help, but were also poor. A religious woman, her one desire was to keep her children off the streets. Barnardo describes how the children were bathed, dressed in clean clothes, given soup, their black curls braided with scarlet ribbons and the mother was found easier work.

Walter (aged19) an orphan: absolutely homeless and friendless: living on the streets since the age of 13. A waif and stray admitted from the London streets in an absolutely destitute condition. Nevertheless amenable to discipline, truthful and honest, showing that all he wanted was a chance.

William (aged 8) a cripple: through the intervention of a correspondent has been received from a poverty-stricken home in a western county. Cannot use his lower limbs: swings along on crutches. When first seen by the lady who applied, he was crawling on the floor, filthy and almost naked. Father dead. Mother epileptic. All relatives in deepest poverty.

Dr Barnardo set up his migration programme, his migrants continually replaced by more and more children flooding in from all over the country. It was expensive and risky to emigrate from the UK in the nineteenth century, and many who would have gone, given the choice, drifted instead to ports and cities, hoping to become part of the new industrial age, hoping new technology would solve their problems. For many, there was success and an improved standard of living, but thousands quickly settled into levels of ingrained poverty from which it seemed impossible to rise. The babies continued to be born. 'London has got too full of children', wrote R J Chambers, to the Select Committee on Emigration.

The mortality rate of newborn babies caught up in the turmoil was 158 in every thousand. Dr Barnardo, who had been a sickly baby, not expected to survive, wrote in 1887: Up until 1884 the 'baby question' met me at every turn ...A Mr Theodore Moilliet left him property which became the Babies Castle with room for 30 babies at a time. He soon ran out of room and began building a new Babies Castle where he could 'gather in all the waifs whom I find deserted and maimed on the very threshold of life'. From 1886 to 1908 the Babies Castle housed mixed infants and babies up to six years.

Dr Barnardo relentlessly cited cases to the public: William M, a boy aged 13. Parents dead. Benevolently sheltered by a sweep. The latter recently married a second wife, a violent, drunken woman, who turned William out of doors...leading a miserable life on the streets, being fed on scraps, sleeping sometimes in a shed or an empty house. Has been driven by hunger to petty thefts. A clergyman writes of him: 'there is nothing against the lad except that he is a waif'.

Kate (aged 9) stone blind: mother a tramp, father dead. Lost sight through severe ophthalmia caught when 12 months old, by sleeping out night after night in severe weather in the streets.

George C a cripple (aged 14) and Philip C (aged 10): father dead: mother weak-minded and for twelve months in a lunatic asylum. Left with five children under 14 years of age. Both boys almost starving.

*L*ines of emigration

Cities seemed evil places to many. Dr Barnardo's purpose was liberating children to send them far away, where England still held sway, but where there was space, sunshine and work. He wrote, '...the lines of our emigration for 1892 have been laid broad and deep. We are hoping, if God spare our lives, and if His servants supply us with the means, to place out in our Colonies this year 600 trained young people. We have the boys and girls, we have the machinery to do the work, we have the experience gained by long years of toil: **WE ONLY REQUIRE THE GOLDEN KEY TO OPEN PORTALS OF THE FAIR LAND OF PROMISE WHICH LIES BRIGHT TO THE EYES OF MANY A BOY AND GIRL RESCUED FROM THE GLOOM AND DARKNESS OF THE SLUMS'.**

15

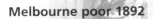

Melbourne poor 1892

The golden key

By 1893, he wrote in the December *Night and Day:* We have, by God's blessing, and His people's aid, taken out of the slums of our English, Scotch and Irish cities, some 24 000 poor and neglected boys and girls who otherwise must have been 'submerged' for ever.

He said: the thick-sown slums send up evil in many directions; physical degeneracy, immorality, drunkenness, squalor, Christlessness...emigration is one of the most potent keys we have to fit the puzzling wards of what we call *our social problem*.

By Barnardo's 50th birthday in 1895, he had worked in the streets of London for 29 years, rescued and sheltered 27 000 wholly destitute waifs, helped 60 781 others by means of ragged schools and migrated 6 805 other boys and girls to Australia, Canada and South Africa. Barnardo even set up a refuge for the children of prostitutes when Jack the Ripper stalked London, (and amazingly was actually a suspect himself for a short time).

The image of this complex man, who has been called a saint and a liar, was of a kind and gentle rescuer of orphans. The reality was that he often fought like a lion to illegally remove children from parents to protect them. He called it, 'philanthropically abducting'. Some parents lived from the immoral earnings of little children who had sexually transmitted diseases. Some relatives violently attacked children in the streets in daylight snatching begged money from them for alcohol. No-one intervened. There was also a concern about family members, crazed and desperate, preying on their children when they were placed in situations, even following them overseas and interfering with their new lives, or writing upsetting letters, so that they slipped back into the position of victim. His philosophy of 'making a fresh start' and 'putting everything behind them' came from rescuing them from 'depraved' family situations. He appeared in court 88 times to defend his actions.

16   Barnardo saw his work jeopardised by relatives, sometimes well meaning but often ill-equipped to rear large numbers of children. Brutalised attitudes of parents towards their children, had shocked Dr Barnardo to the core and he mistrusted parents as a group. They were the enemy. The children had to have a 'clean start'. The Doctor could not rescue the parents as well. Society had made the mothers 'fallen women' or 'undeserving poor'. The men were often absent and not seen as needing help. Children's lives were saved. At first, destitute children could only be handed a cup of cocoa and a blanket. Dr Barnardo fought for funding, and by 1889, could state triumphantly that there were only 61 deaths among 4 642 admittances. 19 604 prescriptions had been dispensed. They were rescued from degradation, photographed, washed, dressed in clean clothes, fed, drilled, educated and given an open door to opportunity.

His overwhelming success in bringing the fates of waifs into the mainstream of British life, meant Barnardo's code of principles was adhered to unchangingly. Although he was undoubtedly right in his time, through the years, some families became victims of Barnardo's earlier stance. In order to give them 'a fresh start', the official line of suspicion of parental motives led to heart-rending separations of children from both their loving parents and foster parents. Parents could suddenly lose their position as parents, while still bonding strongly with their young. Children were sometimes brought in in poor physical condition, terrified of strangers, reinforcing the official line of suspicion of the parents. As late as 1933, the Barnardo's booklet, *Migration and After-care Overseas*, states...'some have relatives whose influence would be definitely hostile or harmful'.

In the *Custody of Children Act 1891,* the British Parliament gave residential institutions the power to 'dispose' of children in situations where a parent had been out of touch with her/his offspring so long as to imply that he/she was no longer interested. A parent's refusal to consent to emigration could be overridden if parents were living off the immoral earnings of the child or had been otherwise abusive.

*O*ut there

There was little questioning about sending them to Australia. In 1892, the Duke of Clarence, addressing Whitechapel lads said, 'there is plenty of room out there, ampler air and larger aims, and here you seem rather crowded'.

The English, comfortably aware of their colonies, regarded migrants as young colonisers, not losing their country, but proudly extending it. Lord Brabazon wrote in 1884, 'Englishmen have to realise that the colonies are not mere possessions but a part of England. Migrants do not lose England when they migrate because Great Britain has become Greater Britain. We have conquered and peopled half the world in a fit of absence of mind'.

'You are forging a fresh link between the Mother Country and the Colonies', Dr Barnardo assured the children.

The British Empire was the largest and most diverse of colonial powers. A new phase of the industrial revolution in the 1870's, had provoked a resolute search for raw materials to feed new industries. Britain and France took the lead with Britain being the more aggressive. The only hindrance to faster colonisation was the difficulty of moving large numbers of people out by sea. The increasingly relentless pace of industrialisation aggravated poverty. This was accelerated by wars and the Depression, so there was always a sea of suffering. Eric Chater wrote of his childhood in the thirties: I was at Epsom for eight years. I can't remember anything before that. I remember my good mum and we were so poor, to get a feed my brother would kick a barrowman in the shins hard and we would run off with some fruit.

17

By 1889, waifs were sought for by agents. Barnardo said, 'a new and healthy environment is more powerful to transform and renovate, than even heredity has been in implanting taint. Purify the surroundings early enough and the taint will rapidly disappear'. The nation nodded its head in approval, thankful waifs no longer plagued its conscience.

As Barnardo migrants enjoyed successs, usually on the land, in Canada, New Zealand and Australia, they invited new chums out, sent donations and dedicated the income of, for instance, the fruit of a favourite plum tree to the Homes. *The Twelve Sheep from Australia*, the story of a yearly donation of sheep from a grateful farmer to the Home that had sheltered him, was sold as a booklet.

'I sympathise with you in all your troubles and I herewith send another 10 shillings' (Ballarat, Victoria, Australia). From a NSW donor, 'Being a Londoner myself, I well know what the misery is that you have to contend with'. Barnardo's were also donated proceeds of a lecture on the Australian bush. *Night and Day,* 1890 describes how £1 600, the cost of sending the first party of 170 boys, average age 15, to Manitoba, was partly paid by a 'generous Australian benefactor'.

Dr Barnardo counted on approval and financial support from the colonies. A letter from the Earl of Aberdeen in Grosvenor Square, London to Sir Henry Parkes, Balmain, Sydney, March 1891: Dear Sir Henry, I desire to commend to your favourable notice the Rev W J Mayers, who with a small company of Musical Boys is about to visit Australia...on behalf of Dr Barnardo's Homes. I am informed that since those Homes were founded 25 years ago, between 17 000 and 18 000 homeless boys and girls have been trained, educated and fitted for their place in life...The Trustees and Committee hope by this deputation to increase the number of supporters of the Homes in the Colonies...

18

Among Australian donors was Big Jim Page, teamster of Barcaldine, Central West Queensland, late MP Queensland and Minister of the Labour Government. From his first wage, he annually sent £10 to Barnardo's. *Four former Prime Ministers were at his funeral in Melbourne in 1921.Ed note.*

In 1891, 500 children in a choir in the Albert Hall sang *Now Lift our Joyful Song*, while bright, fluttering banners proclaimed 'emigration'. The indefatigable Doctor raised funds, appointed agents to scour the streets, answered charges, made speeches, held meetings, personally shopped for rescued children and bought sewing machines for distressed mothers, but directed energy mainly into preparing his charges for overseas homes.

Many lost control of their children. It was easy for offficials to move them out of the country. To facilitate this, both children and parents were sometimes lied to, children given different names or birthdates, making it very difficult to trace their relatives years afterwards.

During the thirties, a matron took two small boys to a room, sat them in a desk, gave them a piece of paper and a pen and said, Alec Topline and Derek Egmore, you are now John Franklin and Eric John Leonard, and write it out twenty times so you don't forget. Eric had been cared for by the Egmores, whom he believed were his foster parents. He later found out they were his grandparents. His unmarried mother's name was Leonard.

At the turn of the century, in both Australia and the UK, some women began to share in the economic boom, although working as outworkers and factory workers conditions were still appalling. However mothers were still especially vulnerable. Deserted mothers could rarely keep their children, who were boarded out, abandoned or kept in a neglected state. Children continued to be at risk. In 1909 in NSW, there was an extremely high illegitimacy rate. The death rate of infants, and the death rate of children boarded out was so suspiciously high that female inspectors were appointed, who could enter any dwelling at any hour.

In 1914 to meet the unrest as a consequence of poverty created by the war, a number of canvas dwellings were made available on the outskirts of Sydney at one shilling and sixpence a week. In May 1914, the Ministry of Labour and Industry made available a Women's Employment Agency, although this did not guarantee employment and was seen as an empty gesture.

In 1918, with the loss of 60 000 Australians, the control of state-aided immigration became a function of the Department of Labour and Industry. From the end of 1914, practically the only state-assisted movement of population into NSW from overseas was with the stated object of uniting families, but clearly, the adjustment was to the new industrial situation. People were battling to stay alive. Children were again seen as part of the workforce, lying about their age to workplace inspectors, abetted by hungry parents.

23

After WW1 there were serious suggestions that a UK 'babyship' be sent to Australia. Doctors expressed concerns to state premiers about affection of bones, muscles, joints, paralysis, syphilis, tuberculosis, fits, ear, nose and throat infections, eye diseases, scarlet fever, measles, chicken pox, whooping cough and heart diseases. The premiers backed away from the idea.

TB, then incurable, accounted for 22% of all male deaths and 26% of all female deaths between 15 and 44 years from 1908 to 1910. The push for immigrants in Australia was further strengthened by concern about imbalance of gender with 38 959 more males than females, more than half of which, (19 313) were in NSW in 1919.

The final step

The first issue of Sydney Real Estate magnate, Sir Arthur Rickard's *Millions Magazine* was the final step in the official sanctioning of child migration in parties to Australia. The slogans were 'populate or perish' and 'immigration our only salvation'. The Articles of the Association declared in part, 'To assist by active propaganda the immigration movement'. In October 1921, the *Millions Magazine* declared Australia must at the earliest possible moment increase her population to 15 or 20 millions.

The first push in 1920, was to offer homes to Britain's 180 000 war widows, as domestic workers for the backblocks. 'Our soldiers have dispelled the British people's misapprehension that we are black or resemble in our physical appearance those other natives of Australia, the kangaroos'. They especially welcomed ex-servicewomen,'they have lost their former shyness and fears of mice, cows and the dark. Their physique and good looks have been greatly improved by their training and work'. There was a less than enthusiastic response to this offer, but by 1920, 283 000 people emigrated from Great Britain, as compared with 147 000 in 1919. Canada took nearly 119 000, and Australia and New Zealand 44 000.

Imperial migration

The Millions Club challenged Australians in the Press with a quiz: Imperial Migration - Questions for Australians:

1. Are you opposed to bringing to Australia or admitting here such of the 180 000 British war widows as can be absorbed as domestic workers on the back-blocks or elsewhere?
2. Are you willing to admit into Australia 60 000 British ex-servicemen to replace the Australians killed in the war, as they can be absorbed without affecting local conditions?
3. Are you of the opinion or otherwise that Australia was over-peopled before the war?
4. Are you averse to having the way made easy for yourselves and others to nominate your friends and relatives to join you?
5. Are you in favour of increasing the female population of the State till it equals that of males?
6. Are you anxious to see Australia's secondary industries fully developed, which is impossible without skilled workers and the capital which always follows immigrants?

7. Are you ready to allow boys to be brought out for farm work under proper safeguards against exploitation, and thus help to keep down the high cost of living and to increase your exports?

8. Are you prepared to see the empty areas of Australia remain unproductive: as, if you do not fill them up with white people and so supply your quota of the world's needs, other nations will come and grow the products for themselves?

9. Are you aware that the offer of the British authorities to pay fares for all the ex-service women and ex-service men you will receive before the end of 1921, is the home Government's offer to help make Australia safe in case of war, and if you do not encourage people to come out now, you must defend yourselves as best you can if threatened at a later date?

10. Are you willing to allow branch orphanages to be established here and so ensure that the money expended on the children is spent in the Commonwealth as it is done already in Western Australia and in Canada?

11. Are you anxious for your country to remain open to attack, heavily taxed, almost devoid of population, comparatively poor and obscure, when you see what population, (even mixed in race and colour) has done for the US, which is a country of equal size, but with twenty times the population?

12. Are you aware that an unpeopled country of proved fertility is more harmful and dangerous to its inhabitants than over-population, and both can be remedied by migration?

People were reminded: 'Australia is not white now. She is empty and being peacefully penetrated by coloured people in the North already'. April 1 *Millions Magazine*: 'Why cannot the Millions Club, seeing that the state government is moving with feet of clay, take up this work. A scheme combining philanthropy with immigration. The cost of upkeep will be approximately £50 per child per annum. The sum required to purchase and furnish the Home will be about £6 000.

The Millions Club members were adamant that migration was necessary to replace Australians killed in the war, plus the immigrants she failed to receive during wartime: 'British emigrants and their descendants, who now constitute the brain and backbone of the United States and the wealth they have created'. The Millions editor commented in 1920 that in the UK, 'workhouses, not to be found in any British overseas Dominion, artificially maintained the employment of some 50 000 poor law officials and that Bumbledom and poverty could be abolished simultaneously by a 'scientific policy of immigration''. Children of a workable age were then considered. Prior to the outbreak of war, money had been allocated from the Dreadnought Fund to assist lads to migrate and settle as agricultural labourers. This was given as a precedent.

25

Bring the boys

A Miss Mabel Cameron, under authority of the Director of Barnardo's Homes visited Sir Arthur Rickard's Millions Club office meeting unexpected enthusiasm. 'Bring the boys to Australia and you will find we will help you right royally', he said. At his request she cabled the London Board and this quietly completed the machinery for group child migration to Australia.

Requests for trained boys and girls throughout the 1890's, from Australia, New Zealand and South Africa had not been met because of the lack of support for them after migration. The Million's Club offered, 'A very suitable home capable of accommodating about 100 boys...secured from the Red Cross Society, known as Scarborough House, Sandringham. An appeal to launch Dr. Barnardo's Homes at Scarborough House brought in £5 000. Gifts in kind included:
Miss E Coghill, Furnishing of one room (valued at £30).
Dr. R. Granville Waddy, Hon. Opthalmic Surgeon.
W.A.Little, Furnishing assistance'. (*Millions*, May 2, 1921)

The Barnardo 'product' was welcomed. Little girls were imbued with moral and religious ideas, trained in habits of neatness, self-help, cleanliness and of usefulness in the way of washing, ironing and mending. Boys were imbued with a strong work ethic and taught trades. They could all read and write and had some competence in music, and respectful manners. Statements from the Millions Club that youth could be moulded to Australian ways, and :'They will learn to be Australian without having to unlearn anything...' perhaps demonstrates desire for a model British type of young citizen.

According to Canon Pughe, Naval Training Chaplain, the successful immigration of lads depends on the four T's - Training, Testing, Transportation and Tending.

The broom or the shovel

In opposition, the Australian Labor Party resolved to offer the most resolute objection to any scheme of immigration 'until every man in Australia has a job or a farm and to cable London to adopt means to prevent further immigrants coming to Australia until work is available for all'. This qualified welcome meant that the child migrants, the brightest and best, several of whom eventually went on to university, or highly successful business, had to work as relatively unskilled farmworkers and domestic servants at the mercy of the system for years. This stated objection relegated many to lose their chance of ever fulfilling their potential, women marrying unsuitably to escape domestic drudgery, men becoming restless and bitter. A minority who were suited to the land, did stay to become successful farmers, especially on dairy farms. The majority of girl migrant workers escaped domestic work as soon as possible.

It was proposed that the boys would migrate in batches of fifty, in the charge of a matron and teacher. The Press said: 'They will be ...guaranteed sound physically and mentally. They will all be war orphans. The cost of upkeep will be approximately £50 per child per annum'. In May, 1921 *Millions Magazine* wrote: 'Cable advice is to hand stating that the first batch of war orphans, boys between the ages of 6 and 10 are on their way to Sydney. We shall receive these boys in their formative years...Then will commence a novel experiment, the Australianising of batches of British orphan children, pronounced physically and mentally fitted for the adoption of their new lives. Mr Percy Roberts, Assistant Director of Dr Barnardo's Homes in London said in his speech on landing, ' These lads have been taught in love and reverence the beautiful in life. They have been disciplined and they come out with big hearts and are determined to make good. To judge from their looks, their alert steps and their general demeanour they are of the right type'.

The Millions Club exclaimed excitedly, 'The natural increase in population (in the UK) averaged one million a year. Consequently hundreds of thousands capable of making ideal Australian settlers were ready to be recruited here. Canada has received 70 000 such children!

The *Berrima* arrived on Monday 24th October, after coming 16 000 miles via the Cape at a cost of £12 000. 'That the *Berrima*, the same ship that took the first body of Australians abroad in the war should bring back to us this first squad of men in the making...', exclaimed the *Millions Magazine*. As the new arrivals marched between files of Abbotsholme College Cadets to Government House, the difference in physique was noticeable. Presents were showered on the newcomers, including new suits of Australian tweed and Commonwealth Government Savings Bank books containing £1.

Sunday Sun:
Barnardo boy from the Great Big Smoke
A shake of the hand - we are all one folk
To-day you stand at the foot of our tree
And leaves and branches are all you see.
But at the foot you will not stop,
For the rosiest fruit grows right at the top.
Here is the trunk, now is the time,
Up with your foot and climb, boys, climb

The *Millions Magazine* of November 1921 showed the Barnardo boys entering Government House grounds between files of Abbotsholme cadets. 'The difference in physique was noticeable and many a heart welled in sympathy for the little strangers'. March 1922, when Sir Arthur Rickard was pressing the Prime Minister for younger migrant children, the Secretary of the Commonwealth Immigration Office in Melbourne wrote to the Prime Minister's Department, 'No objection to our supporting Barnardos. We can get maturer migrants, say youths of 16-19 for fares only and they are immediate producers. Barnardo's boys are not as valuable as these. Therefore unless the government is relieved of all costs and responsibilities except that of contributing fares, I suggest we drop them. In fact it was a proud fact for Barnardo's that the demand for their children always far outstripped the supply. In 1928, 20 farmers applied for each boy and 40 households for each girl. In 1930, Senator the Hon J Daley received advice from the University Club advisors: 'It is my considered opinion that this type of migrant should receive preference over other classes. They are well trained. They come to their adopted country at a tender age and the guiding influence of that great charitable institution, Dr Barnardo's Homes directs their course through life. If the nomination is not approved, we place a 'cog' in the wheel of the institution'.

The Twenties

1921	James H Ireland
1922	Alf and Stan Pollard
1923	Kenneth Gray ❧ Charles Zakharoff
1924	James Hill ❧ Hilda May Gandy ❧ Etta Blane
	Ivy Randall ❧ Dorothy Campion
1925	Fred Dyke
1926	Kathleen Rourke ❧ Ken Surridge ❧
1927	Joe Hammond
1928	Violet Borham ❧ Eva Unwin
1929	James Packer ❧ Henry Gawthorpe ❧ George Beck

AUSTRALIA

Balranald, P&O, England-Egypt-Ceylon-Australia, (one class only), Twin screw steamer, 13 100 tons, 1926 boys party

James Ireland

1921

The first party was seen off by the Duke of Windsor and the widowed Mrs Barnardo. They went to Scarborough House, Sandringham. One of two brothers stowed away and went back to England.

Bill Moverley: I was up at Pelaw Main, near Kurri Kurri in 1988 and I came across James Ireland, who had come out in 1921. I leaned over the fence where this little nuggety bloke was gardening and asked him if he was a Pommie. 'My bloody oath!' He told me he was 10 years old when he came out in the *Berrima*, and went straight onto a dairy farm at Maitland. There were 60 cows to be milked morning and night and only James, the boss and the boss's son, a young lad, to do all the work. James said he went to school each day and got a hiding each night.

30

He told me when he was about 12 years old, a bloke stopped by and asked him if he would like to be a carpenter. James decided to leave the farm. The boss told him he couldn't leave, but he said, 'just watch me'. He learned carpentry and after a time, the carpenter died and James took his place. He built all the wooden houses around about. One day two men in suits came up from Sydney. They asked if he had a ticket to do the work.

James told them there were five houses in various stages of construction and that they should examine them, and if they found one thing wrong, he would stop working as a carpenter.

On Monday 24th October, 47 boys with Mr Percy Roberts in charge, arrived in the P&O steamer, Berrima. Mr Roberts was to model Mowbray Park Farm on Fairbridge, an earlier West Australian home. With a speed of 14 knots, the Berrima carried 350 passengers

The style of miner's cottage built by James Ireland in Pelaw Main

James lived with a kindly landlady, Mrs M Peate. When he died on January 13th 1991, Bill Moverley looked after the burial.

Alf and Stan, (seated), came out in the Benalla on November 19 1925.

Alf and Stan Pollard
1922 and 1925

Alf Pollard's widow, Connie said he did not talk much about his early life, except to say that he wanted to stay and look after his mother and he never wanted to come to Australia. He arrived in the *Moreton Bay* on May 22 1922, aged 11 and went straight to work on a property near Newcastle. The owners left him £500 when they died.

Night and Day, June 1922
                 OFF TO AUSTRALIA
Our Second Barnardo Party For the Fifth Continent

  It was a glorious morning, radiant with sunshine, when we took train for Tilbury to bid farewell to 50 Barnardo boys sailing that day by the *Moreton Bay* for Australia. At Tilbury a labyrinth of railway lines, trucks, and sheds stored with goods confronted us. We sought guidance from the dockyard policeman. 'Where is the *Moreton Bay*?' we asked him. 'Follow the cart', came the laconic reply. A nod of the head and a half-raised arm indicated a man with a hand-barrow a little way ahead. We followed, and soon realised how fortunate we were to have such a guide, for it was a devious route, most difficult to trace unaided.

Alfred was admitted to the pavement outside Buckingham Palace

Alf and Connie were happily married for many years

25th June 1965

TOOK CATTLE TO W. AUSTRALIA

£25,000 CONSIGNMENT

  Mr. Alf. Pollard, of Hill Street, recently returned after taking 30 head of cattle to Western Australia. The cattle were Santa Gertrudis bulls from King Ranch, Bowral, and heifers from "Amaroo" Station, Willow Tree and Coonamble.

  One bull was valued at £8500, and was the most expensive bull ever introduced into Western Australia. The other bull was valued at £1500, and with the 28 heifers the consignment was valued at £25,000. The cattle were delivered to Orleans Farm, Shark Lake siding, Esperance.

  The train trip commenced at Bowral, and continued to Cootamundra, Parkes, where the heifers were loaded, Broken Hill, Crystal Brook, Port Pirie, Kalgoorlie, where the cattle were delivered.

  The purchasers expressed satisfaction with the condition of the cattle when they arrived after the nine days' trip. Mr. Pollard said he did not see one patch of green grass on the long trip. He mentioned that although the train trip took nine days, he returned from Perth to Sydney by jet airliner in five hours.

'Tich' Freeman and Alf Pollard (right), at Crystal Brook 1965

31

Welcoming the Duke and Duchess of York to Maitland

Kenneth Gray
1923

Kenneth Gray was born at Bexhill on Sea in Sussex, England in 1912. In 1921 his father drowned leaving a widow and five children.

Dorothy, his widow, took up the story: Ken was put into Barnardo's, and asked if he wanted to go to Australia. His mother had said he shouldn't go anywhere without his big brother, so they both went, and stayed very happily at Sandringham in Sydney. Brother Tempest, selected Ken to help him run the Sanitarium Health Food Company, Cooranbong, where he was referred to as Ken Tempest. Ken completed the Teacher's Training Course at Avondale and taught at the Primary School, where he met Dorothy, daughter of Pastor J L Smith. In 1936, they were married, leaving immediately for our Mirigeda School in PNG, where Ken was to be Headmaster.

Ken worked in Fiji, the Cook Islands, Tonga, New Zealand and Thailand. He covered up serious health problems towards the end by cheerfulness and a winning smile. Many island folk came to his funeral.

Pastor Ken and other missionaries, including an aboriginal couple and their child, made a daring escape from PNG in February 1942 in the *Diari,* an ancient forty-one foot missionary boat. None were navigators. Travelling behind the *Portrero,* illegally showing a red stern light, they soon fell back with an overheated engine. Alone, with submarines and enemy planes all around, they drifted helplessly. No-one knew Morse Code and only one could read a compass. Limping into Thursday Island, they chose the widest approach, just heavily mined!

Jo was only two when her mother fled with her from the advancing Japanese
Dorothy and Ken leave three children, five grandchildren and one great-grandchild.

Pastor Barnard's family working as missionaries. They and the Grays were the first Australians many of these indigenous people had seen

Ken: The *Diari* was powered by a three cylinder Gardiner diesel, ancient even then - a real joy to start. Each cylinder had to be laboriously pre-heated with a blow lamp. The cylinder of air had to be pumped up to the required pressure, then the flywheel had to be positioned. With cylinders satisfactorily hot, a tap on the air cylinder would be flipped open. With a mighty thump, the compressed air would turn the engine over, and with a shudder, the engine would come to life, perhaps!

In 1933, Ken won more than a week's wages in the Sun's Best Smile Competition

Charles Zakharoff, born Chalva Guigolachvili, as Army mascot, saw his mother murdered by Bolsheviks in what is now Georgia. She died in his arms. Charlie later took part in a Russian film.

Charles Zakharoff
1923

John Ruffels says: Charles, rescued by a kindly British Army Private, Freddy Felks, who saw him taking potato peelings from the Army garbage cans, went with the 99th Artillery Battalion to Turkey as a batman to Captain Fred Elworthy, who had made him the company mascot. A horse rider, he acted as a scout. When the battalion was posted home, Elworthy wangled Charles' entry into the UK, where he was taken to Barnardo's and took the name Zakharoff, given him in jest -'by my Captain'. After an outbreak of smallpox, Charles was taken off the Canadian emigration list and told the Prince of Wales to 'go to the devil', when he visited Barnardo's. But the Prince, on hearing the boy's story, arranged for him to go to Australia. In 1923, Charles came to Australia on the *Ballarat*, with the third official group of Barnardo Boys.

In his flat, Charlie kept a photo of the Prince, another of himself as a boy in a British uniform and a third of 'my Captain', whose grandchildren he had visited in England.

Charles Zakharoff was a noted Sydney cabbie for 60 years, whose 'regulars' included politicians (he shepherded Sir Robert Askin on gambling errands), show business types, journalists, policemen, crooks and conmen. He died aged 89.

In one incident during the 1920's, in Kings Cross, he was challenged and abused by an Italian migrant, who threw a punch at him. Charlie knocked him down. He later read in the paper that he was a gunman who was later shot and killed. 'Luckily I didn't know that when I knocked him down!' he laughed. In the 1980's, Charlie made two journeys back to his native land. Despite having lost the ability to speak in his native tongue, he found relatives from Gori, Tskhinvali and Mejreviskhevi, greeting them with sparkling eyes. John Ruffels asked Charlie if he wanted to be buried in Australia or his native Georgia.
He replied: 'Australia is my home now, all my children are here. I am an Australian citizen. I want to be buried here'. And he was.

33

The Ballarat

Mr Ormsby Gore, Under Secretary for the Churches, speaking at a meeting of the Child Immigration Society, defended state-aided migration, and vigorously defended allegations that boys and girls sent to Australia and New Zealand were ill-treated and exploited...that such allegations were the result of ignorance and prejudice.

Charlie was asked, 'What has Barnardo's meant for you? 'Everything', he replied.

When Jim was dying, he asked, 'have I been a good father?' Esther Dean, his daughter, believes there could not have been a better one.

James Hill
1924

James Hill left his life story for his children, written in the third person, in the name of 'Jim'. He suffered from infantile paralysis causing a deformity in the toes and right thigh, leading to a curvature in the spine in later life. He could not walk until he was four years old. He states that he owes his life to Dr Barnardo, who died the year before he was born, a 'man whose work will never be forgotten'.

He was boarded out aged five in a village in Bedfordshire, in a house where all the water was carried in from a large wooden rainwater cask and the children

clothes and dishes were all washed in a galvanised tub in front of an open fire. His kind old foster mother would put red hot coals in a warming pan and warm the beds.

34

One of his saddest days was when a horse and cart pulled up outside to return him to the Homes. His sobbing foster mother gave him six shillings.

Dr Barnardo's photo in James' bible

The Governor's policy was to rise at 6 am, make your bed, wax the floor and polish it, and shower and parade before 8 am.

At Woodford Bridge, he did not learn a trade because he was semi-literate.

Jim had his fifteenth birthday crossing the Equator, enjoying the ceremonial ducking in the steaming heat. He arrived in Australia on June 4th and after a welcoming ceremony was taken to Barnardo's in Ashfield.

At 8 pm he was taken to Central Station to catch the Temora Mail to proceed to his first job.

The property, 800 acres of wheat, was 416 miles from Sydney on the Lake Cargelligo line. The employer met him on the siding with a horse and sulky.

'Are you the Barnardo boy?'

'Yes'.

'Hell, I asked for a man, not a bloody boy'.

He asked him how old he was. Jim told him he was fifteen.'Ah, well, get in the bloody sulky, and if you're no bloody good I'll send you back!'

James Hill's widowed mother, Sarah, married James Hill, a labourer, who deserted her before James was born in the workhouse. James and his older sister Esther were placed in Barnardo's in 1910, Sarah signing the Canada clause and thereby surrendering any claim she had on her children. At that time she was living on six shillings parish relief and times were very hard, although she was said to be a hard worker and always kept her stove black and the brass polished. James's admission report describes him as two feet high, thin with scattered areas of impetigo. His father was described as having a 'roving disposition', with claims that he ill-treated the mother. The mother 'bears a good character for general conduct and motherhood'.

James' mother Sarah Hill

On his seventeenth birthday he was sent to a 27 000 acre property in the Hunter Valley. The owners were from the old British style of aristocracy. Jim lived in an old unlined tin hut, with two round saplings cut from the bush, nailed to the wall and covered with chaff bags, with a chaff bag stuffed with straw for a mattress. He had his meals, mostly bread and mutton, in the laundry among the dirty washing. He had to wash in the creek and there was no furniture in his quarters. Living in a tent on the property was a Mr Mawson Tindal. He had also come from high society and been educated at Sydney University. He was a very plausible, diplomatic and sympathetic type of gentleman. He was not a great deal concerned with the society he had been brought up in, and was said not to have any respect for their snobbishness. In fact he was more sympathetic to the working class. Mr Tindal had also married into high society and they had owned a large station at one time. However, his wife was very extravagant in entertaining and they had gone bankrupt. His wife had left him with only personal belongings and a tent. He took an interest in Jim and said to him, 'I've been observing for some time how clever you are with your hands. Australia is a large continent and there is a small population for its size. There is a tremendous scope for building construction such as housing and

factories, dams...also in the field of cabinet making. Mr Tindal lent Jim books, put in the balance of money needed to buy a set of tools, and helped him study, so that soon he was being asked to do jobs around the station. Jim was able to repay Mr Tindal by building him a beautiful little dwelling with a verandah, a door and two windows, fitting it out with furniture. Jim eventually bought a block of land and built a workshop on the outskirts of Scone. He made toys and furniture. He hadn't been married long when he lost four fingers of his right hand caught in the twelve inch planing machine. Eleven days later, he got a leather guard made for his hand and went back to work.

In the second world war, Jim served with the Civil Construction Company in the Torres Strait Islands, at times coming under fire.

He became active in the Trade Union movement and for many years was an organiser with the Building Workers Industrial Union. Many hungry men were given food at his home. He was also involved in community affairs having almost single handedly built the Merrylands pre-school.

Hilda May Gandy 1924

Ray Livett, Hilda's son, requested her papers in 1990, when she was in a nursing home. He found out she went into Barnardo's aged nine after her mother became sick. Her father, 'of good character' and health was in the Army .

Hilda came to Sydney in the *Euripides*, in February 1924 and after school was sent out as a domestic.

A typical interior of the day

Miss Wedlock, matron, described Hilda's happy family after they visited her at Picton, in 1939: They drove to Picton in their own car and impressed one as being a very united and happy family. Mr Livett is employed as a carpenter.

36

Dearest Mrs Litchfield.
I am sorry to say that I have not been a good girl lately, but will promise to try to be

& it has made me very tired and cross, & Mrs Tait has been rather upset, because Brian is not very well, & she seems to have grumbled at me quite unconsciously for things I dont know anything about. The other day I had to do three-weeks ironing in one afternoon, & by the time I had finished I was almost dead. I want to know if I am allowed to be left in the house by myself at night time to look after the children till twelve o'clock at night,

Hilda always used to say, 'be sure your sins will find you out'. 'Don't worry, things will be all right in the end'. Hilda always loved babies. She would have liked to have had more to do with the grandchildren but Dad always said when the chicks left the nest it was up to them to fly.

'I'm a good girl I am', was one of Hilda's favourite sayings. Her security lay in pleasing people. This attitude stayed with her from the days of being a Barnardo's domestic.

Ray Livett: Hilda had a hard life. She bore ten children, eight of whom survived, one of whom predeceased her. She had eight grandchildren. She had a full and complete life, always laughing.

Etta's mother was deserted while pregnant with her. A second fiance was killed in France in 1916. Etta was fostered by an 'aunt' because her mother was not well. When it was time for Etta to migrate, the aunt tried unsuccessfully to prevent her departure.

Etta Blane
1924

Etta Blane's story was researched by her daughter, Margaret Booth. Ed.

From a letter dated13th April 1923. Etta's aunt to Barnardos in England:

Dear Madam

I am writing to you in reference to Etta Blane... and I believe it is now time for her to leave the Home as she is sixteen years of age. Her mother, Mrs Ethel Moore of High Street Selbourne is quite willing for Etta to come to me. I hope she has written to you to the effect as she knows Etta will be well looked after and cared for (in fact I brought the child up from birth).

Extract from the Barnardo letter to the aunt:

Etta's mother has given permission for Etta to go to Australia, and had it not been for an out-break of measles she would have gone in March.

Etta is most anxious to go and be

A letter from Etta's mother to Etta in Australia:

Dearest Etta, I am just writing you these few lines trusting you are well. I have heard from the Home that you are going to Australia. Well darling it will be a lovely trip for you and a good start in life. You will be able to come back to us a fine big woman and tell us all about that country, I shall always be thinking of you and you must keep writing to me. I have sent you a little snap of myself it was taken at the last place I was at, me with a cross, cook, kitchenmaid and parlourmaid besides. I hope and trust you will be able to get on better than I have and have your good health, you must always write to your auntie who

has been a mother to you and hope you will come back and stay with her again. Well dearest you will soon have another birthday I will send to you again if you are not gone. Funny you are sixteen then. It does not seem true I have not seen you since you were quite small but I do not forget you and never shall so always feel that I am thinking about you and wondering how you are getting on. So now I think I have said all this time hope to hear from you soon, with all my love and kisses to your dear self from your affectionate mother.

Etta as a teenager wrote to Miss Wedlock, upset at seeing young migrant girls:

Dear Miss Wedlock, I suppose you will get a surprise hearing from me but I was at the fete on Saturday and I saw all those little girls out there, I didn't know they were still coming out. Well I should like very much to take one of those little ones who have nobody so I could write to her for Christmas and birthdays and perhaps take her out sometimes if it could be arranged. So if you could kindly let me know what you think, hoping to hear from you soon, yours truly Etta Blane.

From the Visitor's After Care Report
Mrs Litchfield and I were invited to Etta's home. It is very comfortably and conveniently built and was built by her husband, a builder and is kept very busy in his trade. Etta has a little girl three years old, a very appealing child... Etta and her husband have a happy time.

37

Ivy Randall
1924

Mother, a lady had 'married beneath her'. My charming, handsome father lost all our money. My mother drowned herself in desperation, leaving seven of us.

My grandparents, who lived very comfortably, offered to take the three youngest, but father, with whom they had never been on good terms, refused to separate us  and put six of us in Barnardo's Homes at Barkingside. We never saw father again but I understand that he remarried.

My eldest brother, Edgar, who had been kicked out of home for standing up for our mother, joined the Indian Army. He said, 'Do you know, little sister, you'll be a young lady of nineteen when we meet again!' I didn't see him for fifty years.

We went to the Albert Hall to a musical event. As we filed out, stills of *The Works of Dr Barnardo* were being shown on the screen. I heard one of our  girls behind me gasp. It was an early picture of her on screen in rags, with  dejected eyes. The Minister, pointing at her picture, said, 'Behold the gutter grubs of the world, how they do flourish!' Miss Utton was our cottage mother,

'Granny Utton, leg o' mutton', we little horrors used to call her. She was, I must admit, a little harsh at times, but what a wonderful lady...we were, as we knew full well, a lot better off than girls in other cottages. Miss Utton had many friends in church circles and we were dressed better than other Village girls and went on outings to London and picnics, which these kind friends financed. I was told I was a lovely child with a lot to live up to. Three of us were chosen to sit an entrance exam aged eleven, but none of us could understand the questions and we just sat and looked at the papers.

Our only sex education consisted of being summoned by the cottage mother to be read Marjorie May's *Twelfth Birthday*, a book to prepare us for womanhood, but no-one understood a word and we were glad to escape!

I came to Australia on the *Euripides* in 1924 aged 14 and thoroughly enjoyed myself. I went into domestic service in a big home in Centennial Park where I was treated very well. The Hon Anne McNaughton took an interest in me and told me to 'be a good listener and hitch my wagon to a star'.

Ivy lives in contented retirement on the South Coast.

Dorothy arrived in February 1924 in the *Euripides*. She came to the Dobson family as a sixteen year old domestic and stayed for 74 years.

Dorothy Campion
1924

Isabel Dobson, daughter of the original employers, takes up the story: My mother needed help with three sons and me and Dorothy came as a housekeeper and nanny and stayed on to become a nurse to my parents. From the start she was part of our family and we all loved her. My father left the interest from two thirds of the estate to her and one of my brothers gave her a rent free flat for twenty five years. She was a second mother to me and I still visit her regularly in a nursing home at Pittwater.

Dorothy had been put into the Homes in England as a two year old. She had an 'auntie' who looked after her until she was thirteen and then she was taken and put into a cottage. Her cottage mother was unkind to her, so when asked if she wanted to go to Australia, she said, 'Yes, on the next boat'. She asked for her records when she was with us, read them and burned them. One of her brothers, a chef on a ship, sought her out when visiting

Sydney, but she wasn't interested in seeing him. She never had a boyfriend. She used to say 'I'm only a Barnardo girl'.

Dorothy with her Australian family in 1928. The employer's wife was overseas

Dorothy was still playing tennis at 86 years old with the Careel Bay Tennis Club

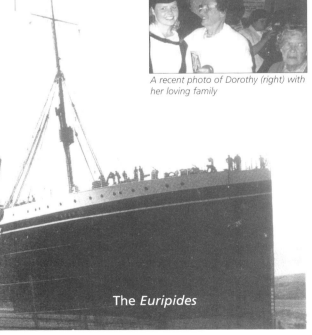

A recent photo of Dorothy (right) with her loving family

39

The *Euripides*

Fred Dyke
1925

Fred, born October 1908, joined the Twelfth Light Horse, Deepwater-Emmaville Troop in 1937 which was originally part of the AIF.

Fred in 1935

Dad died in 1917 leaving mother with five children and pregnant with another, Walter. My mother was a maternity nurse, but battling as times were hard. My father, a foreman, was paid by the week on a big estate, going on to do military training after work without stopping to change his clothes. He caught pneumonia and died.

When mum died, that was the end of our childhood, which up to then had been simply marvellous. We all went into the workhouse at South Stoneham except the eldest and my little sister who was adopted out. I was transferred to Portsmouth Children's Home and stayed there about five years. There were two trades, tailors and bootmakers and a really good brass band. I played bassoon and was going along all right until I played a wrong note. The bandmaster cut the backs of my legs and it really hurt. When I reached sixteen, they put me back in the workhouse. They got in touch with Barnardo's, who took me. At the workhouse, an older man had told me to go to Australia. 'You couldn't do better. You'll have a chance there. It's a wonderful country'.

At Stepney Causeway I felt a sense of justice. When the magistrate asked me did I want to go to Australia, I said, 'I surely do and I'm hoping to be a boundary rider'. He was very surprised. I felt I couldn't get there quick enough.

I was in Sydney for three days, then off to my first job. A Barnardo's person travelled with some of us boys to Singleton. The farmers met us at the railway station. I

Fred with his beloved prize-winning part Arab horse, Three-and-One

went off to a beef stud farm, so I was a boundary rider after all. The owner, a retired Director of a big retail store, used to pay 1 000 guineas for pedigree cattle from England. He was good to me and gave me a lot of responsibility with these beautiful cattle. I had seen my father with horses, so I was happy there.

Fred, is third from left. The photographer at Glen Innes said he had a good profile

Having been in Barnardo's since I was three years old, all my ideas of the future went astray when my two sisters left for Australia.

Kathleen Rourke
1926

Kathleen says: All I wanted was to be with my sisters. Had I stayed in England I might not have had the chance of a

Kathleen, centre, and her two sisters. This photo was used by Barnardo's for publicity

career, but I still had the impression I would be able to attend night classes.

But alas, you were brought out to do domestic service, at a very low wage, and your life was ordered by the people for whom you worked, and it did not include deserting your duties to better yourself. Needless to say, I was not a success and as I grew older grew more and more discontented, and made several efforts to improve my opportunities, but then as now, there was no hope without experience.

When I was 23 years old, and out of the care of the Homes, I took a room and made a quick decision on the spot. I took a course in Book-Keeping and Typing. It soon became obvious I had chosen the right course, and after three months got a temporary position.

This not only gave me experience, but allowed me to earn more money to carry on. My bank balance was getting very low.

The college sent me out to a Chatswood Plumber, whose business was very low at the time, and so was the wage, but I could see if I wanted experience I would have to stay, so fought on. In time, the Boss and I built up the business until we were employing 100

Kathleen in her servant's uniform. When she was studying, she thought of rows and rows of kitchen pots in employer's kitchens. It made her work hard

men and two extra girls in the office. I became part of the furniture in my boss's eyes and it was a shock to him when I fell in love and got married. He still sent costings to me.

I took over the book-keeping again and he eventually made me a director and company secretary.

I started computer courses and was surprised when one played *Land of Hope and Glory* to me! At 86, I enjoy computers and still do some book-keeping.

41

I was born in 1907 in North London. When I was about seven, my father, returned from the trenches in France. He died of war related illness, leaving my mother with five children.

Ken Surridge 1926

Ken's story was researched from fragments of letters, documents and a tape, by his daughter, Jill Morris. Ed

The war widow's pension was not enough. Mother earned money as a cleaning woman. I got little jobs helping at a greengrocers. We moved to Highgate and I remember the clouds all flaming red from the fires in London, and the Zeppelin raids at nightime. I was eventually admitted to Woodford Bridge, Essex. Three of us one night decided to escape, although they treated us very well, but we didn't realise that at the time. I being a very tubby little fellow just couldn't get through the window. On Sundays, the whole Garden Village went to church. The rector had two very sweet little girls and we used to try and sit in the pew behind them because they were our only contact with young females. I was selected to sit for two scholarships and won a place at Chigwell Grammar. One of the matrons, Miss England was one of those old Victorian ladies, very distinguished, sweet and lovable. It was two miles to the new school. Reverend Allen fixed a bike for me by building up the pedals with wooden blocks. As a boarder I wore school uniform plus a bowler hat and a silk topper to church. The Head was keen I should try for a university scholarship.

Note: Mr Kayser, a Canadian, paid for Ken's scholarship at Chigwell. He was unable to pay for Ken to become an Oxford undergraduate, as the headmaster had hoped.

The alternative was Australia and I finally decided to go with my friend, Ron Shelley and his brother. In the course of the trip I got out my bowler hat and I remember flinging it far out to the sea. I was put onto the land, working for a 'Pitt Street farmer', being left on my own for up to six months at a time.   The farm life was not for me.

A pawn ticket receipt for Ken's dinner suit

During the thirties, times were very hard. Ken, like many others, went hungry. For many years after, he suffered stomach pains.   Ken had to sell a very valuable stamp collection given to him by the Reverend Allen.

Ken writes:I became a teacher at Springwood. During the war, I was acting headmaster of Newcastle Boys Grammar, when it moved to Morpeth.

My young life fell apart when mother died in 1925 when I was only 12 years of age. Her death came suddenly at the age of 49 and left me and an older brother alone in the world, father having died in 1920.

Joe Hammond
1927

A FARMER'S LAMENT . . .

It was from England that I came
A farmer's boy to be
To share the life of the great Outback
In this land of the free.

The hours were long, the pay was small
Not like it is today
When all the louts and lay-abouts
Get up and have their say.

The years of toil, became worthwhile
At last I had it made
But it's not as it seems
To really make the grade.

For this is a land of droughts and floods
Bushfires and the like
But even these don't seem so bad
As when the Unions call a Strike.

Their reasons aren't so very clear
And what have we to say?
Not that it matters very much
They'll always win the day.

There's wool to move and freight to shift
But do they give a damn?
The Unions meet and talk and talk
But it's really just a sham.

The talk goes on, and on, and on
But nothing gets much clearer
The only thing we really know
Is that things are getting dearer.

Perhaps some day they'll see the light
And spare a thought or two
For all the folks they really hurt
And that means me, and you

from: *It wasn't meant to be easy! by* Joe Hammond

Joe was put in the workhouse, where he saw,'about twenty middle-aged women walking in pairs around the garden, keeping strictly to the path and they were all dressed in black with white aprons and caps'.

Barnardo's prepared Joe for emigration and he left in the P&O liner Ballarat *of 13 033 gross tons. Five boys travelled in a cabin ten feet by seven*

On his second day in Sydney, Joe was put on a train to a mixed farm at Boggabri. 'Up at 5am milk the cows, and work through till 7pm, for ten shillings a week'.

Joe joined the Army and after the fall of Singapore found himself in Changi Square. 'The work...after the long hours on the farm, was more of a holiday'. In three and a half years as a prisoner, Joe was only struck twice by a guard.

Joe went back to Boggabri, to the farm where he had started work and bought it. In the end he spent about 45 years on the same property.

Joe said: I was considered a bit of a dill at school and was never in the top ten but often in the bottom five, but this generally makes us try harder. We can't all be whiz-kids, but most of us make the grade eventually.

43

Violet Borham
1928

I was put in before the age of two, mother had died leaving four children with nobody able to look after us except our elderly grandparents.

My father, Boots at a hotel, had a good job, but spent too much money on alcohol. Mother had to go out to domestic work and she worked a week in wet clothes, caught pneumonia and died. On the day of mother's funeral, my father jumped off Exeter Bridge, was rescued by a postman and was put in prison for attempting suicide.

I understand he married again after he came out of prison. My sister was 13, then there were two brothers, one of whom went to Canada, and then me, aged two. I was put in during December, 1913, on a Saturday and on Monday I was boarded out to an elderly lady who had brought up eight Barnardo boys. Mrs Grimwood was a marvellous lady, she couldn't do enough for you. At 12 years of age, I was recalled to Barkingside to train as a domestic. I would liked to have been a dress-maker. It was hard work, but although I'm small, it didn't worry me. Girl Guides delivered notes all around the Village asking if anyone wanted to go to Canada and I wanted to go and did all the examinations, but the day the party left, I was in hospital having my tonsils out. You mustn't have anything wrong with you and you didn't have a say. During the examinations, the girls would cluster round the doorways asking, 'Did you pass?' The next note the Guides brought round asked if we'd like to go to Australia. I went through the examinations again. 100 sat but only 32 passed.

PT on the Berrima. *During rest time in the* Berrima, *one girl sneaked our records. I read mine. It said 'no brothers or sisters, mother dead, father committed suicide'*

Aged seventeen, I was working at Summer Hill in Australia.   I dressed in my best but when my employers saw me they said, 'We asked Miss Wedlock for a big, strong girl, oh well, you'll have to do'.   You just had to take whatever was dished out, you never answered back.

At Summer Hill, I received a letter from my brother asking me to write and tell him about my life in Australia. I wrote to the Governor at Barnardo's, saying I didn't know I had a brother, finding out he had been in Canada since he was eight years old.   I then found out I had another sister and brother. They kept in touch with father, visiting him in hospital before he died. He asked for 'the little maid', (me).

I think Dr Barnardo needs re-congratulating - the grateful thanks from thousands - he's got mine.   They are the largest family in the world and I'm part of it. If someone walks through my door and says they are from Barnardo's, I will share anything I have.

The Thirties

1930   Henry Wheeler ❦ George Barraclough

1931   No arrivals

1932   Eric Dodge

1933   Dermott Reilly ❦ Myfanwy Shapland

1934   Jack Smith ❦ Bill Moverley ❦ Bill Webber ❦
      Vi Coughlin ❦ Ben Rhodes ❦ Eileen DeVere ❦
      Tom Blake

1935   No arrivals

1936   Tony Edwards ❦ Jessie ❦ Enid ❦
      Dennis Downham ❦ John Buxton ❦ anonymous

1937   Irene Dando ❦ Ken Church ❦ John Bown ❦
      Ted Burns ❦ Henry Gerstle ❦ Ruby Penney ❦
      Roger Slaughter ❦ Peter Chaffey ❦ Marjorie Marchant ❦

1938   No arrivals

1939   Robert MacCaughan ❦ Peter Crosse ❦
      Mary Allison ❦ George Hurdle

AUSTRALIA

The *Ormonde*

Mother abandoned me aged four. As there was not a father, I went to the Woodstock workhouse in Leicester. I was fostered until aged seven, then sent to Stepney Causeway.

Henry Wheeler
1930

On admittance, a child's clothes were taken, they were given a good hot bath and scrub, given new clothes and their picture taken.

Aged seven

I was in Boys Garden City until I was aged ten. In 1930, I was chosen to go to Australia, in the *Balranald*. We were the second group to arrive at Mowbray Park, where life was great, discipline was very strict, we used to get our share of canes across the backside, but we all settled down to the farming routine and as we grew older, were given more responsibilities. I made many friends, most of whom have passed on, but life in general was very good. The most traumatic time of my life was aged 14, leaving the farm and my mates and going out to a strange environment. At my first job I was not treated very good, I did not eat with the family, given all the hardest tasks, and worked 16 hours a day seven days a week. After three months I left and my next two places I was treated as family. All in all I thank Barnardo's for the strict upbringing, it has stood me well in all my years.

In 1939, I joined the AIF aged 19, with the 2/4th Battalion 6th Division earning the rank of Sergeant and serving in New Guinea, North Africa, Greece, Crete , Syria, Lebanon and Palestine, where I met my future wife. On discharge, I went into the building business. In the ten years postwar we had four daughters. In 1955 we migrated to the USA, as my wife had family there. I immediately got settled and started working in construction. I did very well, and was able to put our girls through college.

It wasn't until papers and records were open to us that I realized that I must have family. When I received papers from the After Care in Sydney in 1983 my admittance card showing my grandfather and mother lived in Deddington, I took it on myself to write to the Deddington address knowing that it was a very long shot because the address was from 1927. To my shock and amazement, I received a letter from the local printer that his father knew the Wheeler family that used to live there and that I had a brother living in Kenilworth and that my mother was still alive. He forwarded the address of my brother and we immediately got in contact. It is a very long story of our finally meeting and missing my mother by three months. I found many more family and have many pictures. I researched my family tree through the Oxfordshire Archives, tracing my family back to the late 1600's.

Henry, happy and successful in Colorado

I went into Barnardo's aged about six years. I don't know the circumstances and I've never tried to find out. I now know my parents and sister are deceased.

George Barraclough
1930

I came out in the *Balranald* in 1930 and went to Mowbray Park Farm School when Mr Shoebridge and Mr Heath were there. I only got one belting, for pinching fruit off a tree. Mostly I have very happy memories of that time. We swam, fished for eels and the market gardener and his wife made a bit of a pet of me.

I went up to Grenfell to a mixed farm - cattle, sheep and wheat. Times were hard in the thirties but the employers were good to me. I ate with the cook and the sharefarmer. I had my own hut with a kapok mattress, chair and table and fireplace. I could boil up the billy and make tea if I wanted.

I stayed on the farm until 1941, then joined up. I went with the 2nd 1st Survey to Syria, Lebanon and Egypt.

After the war I trained as a painter and decorator and this became my trade. I got married to my first wife in 1947 and unfortunately she died.

I have been happily married to my second wife for 25 years.

George in 1946

We were were well-dressed and well-shod and well-fed, better than many kids in the thirties.

HELP
-the Child
-the Farmer
-the Nation

Young British Empire Builders
FOR AUSTRALIA

51

Eric Dodge
1932

It was the love of the sea that caused me to volunteer to come out. I was interested in ships and I found out which was the furthest away, and asked to go to Australia so that I would have the longest trip...

Born in Croydon, Surrey, England in 1922, it was 1932 when I was chosen to migrate to Australia. I arrived in the *Balranald*, in November. At the outbreak of world war two around 1940, my mother wrote and told me I was a child of incest. He was a drunk,

owned a pub but lost it. Kicked my mother out, she was seventeen and relatives took the others but wouldn't take her. She nursed me for nine months in a home for unmarried mothers and fostered me until I was eight, when I went into Barnardo's at Stepney.

Aged eight on admission to Barnardo's

I loved my mother very much and was always grateful to her. We were able to write and she sent me presents. I wasn't very strong as a child. Once they counted one hundred and fifty boils all over my body.

Aged ten and Australia bound

I was fostered with a Mr and Mrs Royce with some other boys for about two years, in a pretty village called Wetheden in Suffolk.

Eric and friends

When I was about nine years old, a lady came to school asking if anyone would like to go Australia or Canada. Some months later I was at Woodford Bridge. My first impression of Picton was 'dreadful' arriving in a freezing cold winter.

'If the King can call me Captain, so can you', said Captain Rees. I took a rainbow gobstopper to bed once and it must have got stuck in my throat when I was sleeping because they found me lying there bright blue and Harry Cornwell thumped me on the back and brought me back to life.

As part of farming life we learned killing. Two of us had to catch a pig, whack it on the snout, cut it's throat and drain the blood into a basin. We worked long hours, with an hour for lunch, keep and ten shillings a week. I slept in a hut made of packing cases on a concrete base. Mr Ladd took me away because the life was too hard. My Estonian employer had to get men to replace me and pay them £1 a week. Five men came and went in quick succession.

I have good memories of the Homes - where would I have been without them!

My mother came to say goodbye. 'Don't cry Eric, we'll see each other again'. 'But you won't know me', I sobbed, 'I'll be all black!'.

I worked at Girraween for a Baptist Minister with a poultry farm who didn't take a stipend in the Depression. He was a good man.

Joining the Merchant Navy, I went round the world eight and a half times, working first as a steward, then as an anti-aircraft gunner and watchman on the bridge. I saw my mother on June 10th 1932 and again exactly ten years later on June 10th 1942. She and a friend were working at the Stirling aircraft factory at Swindon. I had a chance to go on the liner *Ceramic* but I had only just met up with my mother and didn't want to hurry back. The *Ceramic* was sunk with all hands except one in the South Atlantic. My life was spared for a reason, I became a Minister.

✝

I feel compassion because I had lived a life before joining the church. I was even in prison for two days in New Zealand. I jumped ship because I wanted to marry a girl I was keen on. I was going to sail to Australia from New Zealand in a small yacht, the *Pioneer*. A friend came with me. We only got up the coast a bit and we got stuck. We wanted to avoid the police but we got hungry, gave ourselves up and spent two days in jail at Mount Eden. I have visited Goulburn prison as Chaplain. When the inmates tell me I wouldn't know how awful the conditions are, I think, 'I've got more idea than you

know'. When I finally got back and rang the girl, she said 'Eric who?'

Being in the Ministry, I didn't have the funds to visit my mother. Our church congregation found out that I hadn't seen her for 37 years and collected enough for my dear wife Betty and myself to go over.

Mother never married but had a happy life. She and a lifelong friend worked together as cook and maid for years.

53

Eric and his mother, proud of each other

Barnardo's 1933 Party in the Barrabool

*Front row: Kenneth Saunders Harold (Tich) Freeman Bertie Chamberlain
Norman Fullerton Lenny Bridle Oswald (Ossie) Davies Lesley Lee Edward Fletcher Thomas Elliott*

*Backrow: Charles Apps Clyde Davey William Isaacs Edward Irving
Leonard Noyce Derrick Allen Bill Robbins Leslie Paxton Tom Duffy (D'Arcy) Thomas Alexander William Alexander
Bill Copus George Screen John Harris John Savage Dermott Reilly   Standing: Mr Gregg Jack Hayden*

Born in Dublin, Ireland, I was put into Barnardo's aged six. I don't remember any family and believe my life started then. I was moved to England to various homes and in 1933, was chosen to migrate to Australia.

Dermott Reilly
1933

I completed my Qualifying Certificate at Mowbray Park Farm School. In 1936, thanks to Captain Rees, who fought for me and instigated it, I entered Hurlstone Agricultural High School and boarded from 1936 to 1940 inclusive, returning to Mowbray Park Farm at weekends and school holidays.

I was school captain and captain of the 1st XV which in 1940 were competition premiers. I was selected in the Combined High School's 1st XV Rugby Union team and appointed captain. In 1940, I was vice captain in the 1st X1 cricket team. I represented the school at the Combined High School's Carnival in the one mile event and in the NSW School Boy's Athletic Carnival, in the 880 yards event, gaining second place, and also reached the boxing finals.

After matriculation and Sydney University, I won a scholarship to Armidale Teacher's College

experimental grass

I served in New Guinea in the AIF from 1941 to 1946. I completed a post-war degree in Agriculture at Sydney University in 1950, and my Masters degree in 1961, the thesis being on research into golf and bowling green diseases. While at University I played Rugby Union in Reserve Grade and Ist XV.

I assisted in setting up the Australian Turf Grass Research Institute during 1950 - 1960. I lectured at the School of Agriculture and Horticulture, Department of Technical Education, leaving in 1961 for private enterprise, working with a range of companies specialising in agricultural chemicals, including Roche Ltd., where I was Technical Manager/Director.
I spent three years before retiring in 1987 as an independent agricultural consultant, specialising in crop protection chemicals.

55

*In 1956, I wrote regarding the retirement
of Miss Dobbie and Miss Warrell, 'I take pride in
having known them since they first arrived at
Ashfield and it's only when one has children of one's own that
one realises the difficult task they have have over 20 years.
Together they have indeed done a noble service for their many
children who came from England to make Australia their home.
They have always encouraged the girls to make Australia their
homeland, to be proud of it and to learn to love it, my very
early recollections of Miss Dobbie are the times I sat listening to
stories of the early pioneering families of Australia and the
hazards and difficulties they faced. If they achieved nothing
else at that stage of my upbringing, they certainly sowed the
seed of 'love of country'. Whilst arguing that there is no
substitute for the family circle, and in particular a mother...both
Miss Dobbie and Miss Warrell made excellent substitutes. If we
required affection we were given it, and many were the trials
and problems that I took to them. Personally and with their
wisdom and guidance, these problems, however trivial were
ironed out or were made to be seen in their true perspective:
there is little more we could ask of parents.*

Myfanwy Shapland

As an eight year old, I always liked geography. My teacher pointed to Australia on the map and I suddenly realised I was going a very long way.

Myfanwy Shapland

1933

In 1986, when I received my Admission History, I found out that I was illegitimate. My putative father was said be a Russian Jew, who worked as a tailor, my mother a domestic servant of 'good general character'. My mother, who was not robust, placed me in a good foster home in Kent. She worked in the centre of London. She found it very difficult to manage and when I was six years and ten months, gave me to Dr Barnardo's although the report says she was very attached to me. The Admittance Report states: 'The mother has worried a great deal over the welfare of her child and is willing to contribute towards support when admitted'.

I was often sick as a child, small and weak and I became two years behind at school because of ill-health. When my papers arrived, there was a strange little unsigned handwritten note amongst them which read, 'Myfanwy Shapland, Mother very attached but not well off or very robust. Why was she sent to Australia ?
The matrons were all very kind to me. Matron Dobbie always praised me and gave me special food from the table.
I received a legacy of £200 from Matron Gertrude Begg.

Dear Madam,

I am sure you will be glad to hear that we have received a cable saying that our party of children have arrived safely in Australia after a splendid voyage.

I enclose a photograph of your daughter which was taken just before she sailed, and which I am sure you will like to have.

Yours truly,

Will you send [illegible] any of those photos of you [illegible] the ones you took of [illegible] when I was in Canizzaro as I have lost the one you gave me of me when I was a baby. I gave matron my bible to look after for me and I still have my Christening flower in my bible. Well I hope you had a happy Easter.
Goodbye till another time

I joined the WAAAFs, serving in Australia during WWII. After the war I received a BA at Sydney University and Dip Ed at University of Canberra and became a high school teacher, marrying a research scientist in 1951. We had four children and are so proud of their achievements. Two attained Masters degrees in International Law, and another is progressing towards a Masters in Commerce. My son is in the Defence Department.

Jack Smith 1934

I walked up to a little tenement house, one of many in rows in Belfast. The three girls who had been so kind, Kathleen, Mary and Maude, all recognised little Harry. 'Oh, Harry, we always knew you'd come back', said the eldest through her tears. I took them all to the best hotel, gave them one thousand pounds each and walked away.

When we were taken to Liverpool and then on to Picton, none of us knew what was happening. When we landed, on October 25th, 1934, from the *Barrabool,* the heat was astronomical. We went to Thornborough House. I was nine. By the time I was ten, half a dozen of us could harness the horses and take the dray to chop wood. Each year we went to Wollongong, and one day at the baths pool with some Home's kids, I was sitting on my own when a man in a suit asked me, 'Are you Harry Sloane?' I just stared at him and he went away. I have often wondered who he was because no-one in Australia knew me by that name.

Picton

My first job after leaving Picton in 1942 was on a dairy farm near Dapto, NSW. I earned seven shillings and sixpence and my keep, working 13 hours a day six days a week and six hours on Sundays. After one year I moved to a sheep and wheat property in the New South Wales town of Trundle. Here I learned to shear and crutch sheep and work a team of 12 horses pulling a 12 disc undercut plough. I'd go into the flock, pick out a wether, put it into the back of the sulky, travel back to the homestead to kill and dress the carcass and hang it in the meat safe.

In 1944 whilst still at Trundle I volunteered to join the Army. Although I passed my fitness test with flying colours I was informed by the Medical Officer it was doubtful I would be accepted as I suffered from a terrible stammer. I went to Sydney for the final decision on my intake and was advised that as they were getting short of troops in New Guinea, I would be accepted. They immediately sent me to Canungra for jungle training. On our final bivouac we passed O'Reilly's Guesthouse and the guests yelled to us with excitement 'The war is over!'

The war was officially over, the Army required six volunteers to join the War Graves Commission. Although there were thousands of troops training at Canungra, I was lucky enough to be selected as one of the volunteers! The Commission shipped us off to Singapore, our duties here being unknown. One morning it all became clear. Our OC, Major Ron Kerr, asked if anyone could signwrite. I stuck up my hand, was made a Corporal sign writer and doubled my pay from fifteeen shillings a day to one pound ten shillings a day even though I had never painted a letter in my life! In nine months I successfully undertook the inscription of 9 800 War Graves at Kranji War Cemetery in Singapore.

Lord knows what would have happened to me - thank God Barnardo's picked me up.

I was picked off the streets of Belfast, put in a big, black car and taken to the 'ever open door'. I was known as Harry Sloane when a youngster. My mother was Dorothy Smith. A friend of my father's, Harry Sloane, looked after me and I was named after him. He had three teenage daughters who were all good to me. In the Depression, they each worked one day a week at the Belfast linen factory but they used to buy me fish and chips on pay days.

While in PNG, I met a young bloke who was goldmining in Wabag. He had started prospecting in uncharted country. I chartered three light aircraft - Dragons. We took timber up, for sluice boxes, diverted the river and worked the creek, for gold and platinum. We took tomahawks, beads, salt and mirrors to trade for 70 carrier boys and sweet potato to feed them. Unfortunately there was a bad harvest and the pile of sweet potatoes was much smaller than we wanted, so there was grumbling and it was dangerous. The interpreters told us there had been a couple of murders the week before. We were unknowingly only a couple of miles away, as the crow flies, from the biggest goldmine in the world, Porgora.

£ £ £ £ £ £ £ £ £ £ £ £

I returned to Lae penniless but full of ideas. I painted houses and buildings with the help of over 100 natives - a special formula of paint which resisted fungus. It was made up partly of zinc oxide, and lead titanium. I had cracked a formula which was heavily in demand, so I started NG Paints.

I was in PNG for 27 years. I had 100 people working for me. I looked after my native workers the best way I knew, 'number one man belong paint', they called me. When I left, I gave the business to my foreman. He came from County Cork, but I didn't hold that against him.

Jack Smith (left) and Harry Cornwell, the sports master, who transferred from the Army to the Air Force and survived 64 sorties and was our hero. The average for an airman over enemy territory was eight. Harry is now in his ninetieth year and fit and well

59

I was one year old when my father was killed in a mine explosion, my mother receiving nothing in way of compensation.

Bill Moverley
1934

Six years old

I went into the Babie's Castle and was fostered out from Barnardo's. I used to be put into a suit to sing, sometimes at St Paul's Cathedral, London. Years later, Norman Fullerton saw my photo and said, 'Hey, that's my suit'. He'd been fostered out to a tailor who'd made him a made-to-measure. I was ten when I came out to Australia in the *Barrabool*.

I am on the left in the photo, wincing from the pain in my back. I ran away after a beating and a man in a pub said he'd take me to the police station, but he drove me back to the farm and I was given more cuts with apple sticks. 55 years later, Gerald Griggs, John Humber-Stone and I met up again

Barrabool

Bill

I was offered a carpentry job at Fairbridge and ended up at Molong. I was recalled from the Army when I came back from the Middle East. The war meant a shortage of staff. There were only two cottages, no bathroom.

Colonel Heath, the only man who ever rose from the ranks to join the Grenadier Guard's band was sitting quietly one day having a cup of tea, when there was a sound of music, drums. The whole band marched in and surrounded him, playing a fine tune.

Ben at Luna Park

Ben Rhodes Tom Griffiths Harry Unwin George Hundine and Mrs Hundine

After I was married, someone told me to put in for a soldier's settlement block. I said why, I've never won anything. I got such a shock when I won a block 25 miles out of Orange. When we got there and saw the 850 acres, I wished I'd never set eyes on the place. There were no fences and thousands of rabbits everywhere. We poisoned 7 000 a week at one stage.

I started with a shovel, pick, crowbar, cross-cut saw and share of a tractor. There was no house we had to build one. We had 28 quid a month to live on. We used to cart water from the creek and leave it overnight in a barrel with epsom salts. We had kerosene lamps. We had a tin hut at first, the nearest neighbours were two miles away. We all chummed together and built a gravel tennis court where we met as a social event. We had three kids and my wife was expecting. One day she heard the kids yelling and she saw a tiger snake chasing them.
She knew you never take your eyes off a snake, so she kept her eyes on it, felt around for an axe and ran and chopped it's head off. Eventually we had poultry and I went shearing and built shearing sheds.

65

Eileen DeVere
1934 (Henderson)

Born in Belfast in 1922, I was one of five. Here with George, (top) who went down with the *Phoebe*, and Maurice, later a specialist in Roman and Suffolk history

My mother took me and my two youngest brothers by the hands and through the 'ever open door', in 1931, saying we would only be there for a few days. Consequently I was always taking my brothers by their hands and trying to take them back through the gates and home again.

After my parents split up, my mother told me my father had died. On the admission form it stated he had a 'paramour'. Mother remarried and died in childbirth in 1940. One of my brothers still living with my father, who

was not dead at all, wrote to me in Australia when I was sixteen, and told me the truth. I had very good written contact with my father until he did die but I never saw either parent

Eileen aged 12

again after being taken to the Home. I wanted to go back after the war but with my own family it was too difficult. I came out in the *Balranald* in 1934 and went to Ashfield. I attended Burwood Domestic Science School and studied domestic science, there was no other choice. Before I had turned fifteen I was a domestic servant on a property, ten miles both ways from anything at all. There was no electricity and the work was heavy and constant, washing clothes in the copper, chopping wood for the chip heater, cooking, sewing,

cleaning and darning in my little brown dress. I longed for the day when I was twenty-one. On my half day off, I wrote letters home on the corner of the table. When the war broke out, the government brought in woman power and there were no servants any more. I was liberated! I was a machinist in a parachute factory, the Light Aircraft Company, in Grace Brothers, Broadway, Sydney, which was a delight. I worked with country girls who had all come to the city in search of work. I had a room at Summer Hill, ate out, (we weren't allowed food in our rooms), often fish and chips. I made lots of friends and we went roller skating and dancing at the Trocadero.

Sadly, brothers George and Norman were killed in WWII.

I married and had seven lovely children and now there are 12 grandchildren and one great- grandchild.

I win many first prizes for my crochet work

With my sister, Clara in England

I don't know anything about my family. I was nine years old when I went in.

Tom Blake
1934

I was at Kingston. It was a magnificent edifice with roomy grounds managed by Mr Gardner. Some claimed he was a tyrant but in truth he was a strict disciplinarian and needed to be, with 150 boys of all ages to control. The home boasted a large orchard, a veggie garden, which supplied Kingston and other Homes, its own school, gymnasium and hospital.
He organised the well known pipe band to lead the scouts and cubs to church. Being a cub leader, I was privileged to carry the flag. The local people would come and cheer the parade.
I wasn't asked about going to Australia, just sent, but it was exciting in the *Barrabool*.

After Mowbray Park Farm School, I went onto a sheep station at Bathurst, where I was treated like one of the family.
I saved up my money and went through Sydney University and became a postgraduate at Melbourne University in engineering.

I have three lovely daughters and five grandchildren. All the children are doing very well and one grandson is the dux of Penrith High School.

Kingston Naval Training School

67

Ken was seven and I was nine, living happily with foster parents. A cruel blow, we were never to see those loving foster parents again and I was not allowed to say goodbye to Ken.

Tony Edwards
1934

Within two days of arrival at Stepney Causeway (No. 12 I think) Ken and I were split up and I found myself in Liverpool at the Myrtle Street Dr Barnardo's Overseas Training Branch.

Major Roberts was the Superintendent with a staff, all strict disciplinarians. No love was wasted between Mr Elliot, Mr Atkins, and certainly not Mr Molyneau, and the boys. I guess it was just the times we lived in, but a real shock to this nine year old. I was glad to go anywhere away from Myrtle Street, Liverpool. I recently returned and stood staring at the brick facade of the institution where I was from 1932-4. A caretaker asked me why I was photographing a brick wall and commented that I must have been there in the 'gruel' days. I don't remember 'gruel' but I remember 'cruel'. My introduction to that place, was from a little village in Suffolk, where I was loved and cared for. They put your arms and legs inside your nightshirt and slid you around on the floor and then put your head in the toilet and flushed it. The Master in charge had a split belt he called his 'Willy Willy'. He used to dangle it in front of you before you got cut. I think he was a sadist. I walked passed a room once and some of the older kids had him under a pile of mattresses. They yelled at me to get lost if I knew what was good for me. I think they were trying to kill him. We could all read and write.

The police used to come to the outside school I attended, St Lukes with meal tickets for three meals a day. We were a lot better off than many others outside.

I used to deliver pamphlets for Oswald Moseley supporters, not knowing what they stood for, at half a crown a time. They used to meet in different houses wearing black jumpers and grey strides.

In late 1933, I was selected to go with a party to the Prince of Wales Farm School on Vancouver Island, Canada. We would have been the second party to the new school. Previously, most boys from Myrtle Street were sent direct to employment when sixteen or seventeen years old. Once more fate intervened and I finished up in the Liverpool Infectious Diseases Hospital with Diphtheria.
When seventeen weeks later I emerged, I had missed the party to Canada. Fate how I love you, for in April, 1934, I was the only boy from Myrtle Street in a mixed party of thirteen boys and nine girls, from many different orphanages in the UK, outward bound to Kingsley Fairbridge Farm School, Pinjarra, Western Australia, in the *Ballarat*. We arrived on May 15th.

The school was a village of cottages and life was good under the strict but fair control of Colonel Heath. With him was

The *Ballarat*, built in 1921, broken up in 1935, was used by several early emigration parties

In 1932, my foster brother, Ken Church, and I were recalled back into the Barnardo system. We had enjoyed a wonderful life, in my case since fourteen months of age, with loving 'parents', John and Alice Clarke, in the little Suffolk village of Southolt.

Mrs Heath and their adult daughter, Elsie, who ran the village general store, the source of all 'goodies'. 'Bonk' as the Colonel was affectionately known by us all, unfortunately left us, late 1936 or early 1937, to take

THE SOUTH-WESTERN SECTION
WESTERN AUSTRALIA.

over a new school, the Northcote Farm School, Victoria. In 1936 I had a unique experience. Our cottage was named after Isaac Newton, the next Douglas Haig. Talking one day, the subject was mumps. Harry Olsen, from Haig said the best dose he'd ever seen was a kid named Ken Church in Lucking House at Boys Garden City.

Kingsley Fairbridge, the Oxford graduate who designed and built the Farm School for the Child Emigration Society, later the model for Mowbray Park Farm School

After quizzing Harry what this kid looked like, I had reason to believe this kid was my foster brother, Ken. I wrote to Captain Leuwin at the Boys Garden City with an explanation of times and dates. You can imagine my joy when some months later, almost simultaneously, I received a note from Captain Leuwin in the UK, and, one from Captain Rees at Picton, enclosing a letter from Ken who had been migrated to Picton, NSW, in 1937. We were yet to meet.

Funny, when kids in Suffolk, I being the bigger always rode in the billycart, while Ken pulled. We had to gather hogweed to feed our caged rabbits which Mum made into wonderful pies. Ken often said 'one day when I'm a soldier and you are a sailor', (it was always going to be that way even in those early days), 'I'm going to bash you for this'. Thank goodness in January, 1941, Ken had either forgotten or forgiven me. In January, 1941, *HMAS Hobart* was serving in Australian waters prior to going to the Mediterranean in June and outside Wynyard Station in George Street, Sydney, by prior arrangement, I met this huge fella in a Tanky's battledress, part of the Australian Armoured Division. Ken Church and I were finally reunited and have stayed close ever since.

69

Jessie ~ 1936

When I was six and Jimmy, my favourite brother was ten, Dad took us to Stepney Causeway.
He didn't tell us he was going to leave us there. I screamed and screamed then they took Jimmy.

Happier times

My father, the Silver Plate man in the Victoria Hotel, London, all found and £2 a week, married my mother who already had six children.
I remember her singing and playing the piano and buying jugs of beer on Sundays. She ran off with someone else. At Barnardo's I cried for a fortnight. They dosed me up with castor oil and dressed me in a navy dress with a red stripe. The saddest time in my life was when I was taken from my foster home in Wiltshire, a lovely family. The doctor said I had knock knees and curvature of the spine. I went to the Girl's Village Home.
Aged twelve, my brother Jimmy went to Watts Naval Training School, but they found he was colour-blind, so he enlisted in the Army. As an officer in the Dunkirk retreat, he had to shoot a man whose legs had been blown off.
I turned 15 at Naples on the way out. After four days at Ashfield I was sent to a large Canberra household where from the moment I awoke and put on my navy uniform to the time I fell asleep, I worked. They spoke nicely to me, but I only had half a day off on Thursdays if I finished my work. One Sunday, I was hysterical. My employer put me on her bed and called the doctor. He put an ammonia swab over my nose and asked me if I knew any boys - they thought I was pregnant.

70

Enid with Jessie at Port Said on the way to Australia

I had three months off and then returned to domestic work. Girls I spoke to at church were in the public service. I thought I would try and sit the exam. I was offered a temporary position. A friend, Vi, wanting escape too, talked herself into a junior reporter's job at the *Canberra Times*. I shared a room with her. She got a good salary and they gave her a bicycle.
The girls at church would say, 'Why did they send you out, there aren't enough jobs'. It was hard. I managed to get a position as a public service filing clerk. At 18, I had my own room. Barnardo's, at first unaware of my independence, were pleased that I was settled and a success.

I have a son and two lovely grandchildren. Barnardo's filled the bill for me but I thought it was wrong not to be notified when my father died nor given any explanation about being taken. I felt I was being punished for something. I was happily married for 39 years, to a government printer. I had £380 in the bank when we got married and he didn't have anything!

I have lived at Bondi Beach all my life, and I love it!

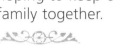
Enid and sister Vera

Mother died when I was six, the eldest of three children. Father, a civil engineer had to travel a lot. He married an aunt, hoping to keep our family together.

Enid ~ 1936

My father, Leonard in the St Johns Ambulance Brigade

Enid at 9 months

My mother, Maude Johnson was a Red Cross nurse in WWI. She had TB

The Home's library

Jasmine Cottage. Miss Marsh and her girls

Camping July 1935

We went on holidays and the day we returned, I heard my aunt say, 'the children will have to go'. The youngest was adopted and we two went in. My stepmother later died and my father wrote to me up until WWII.

I was taken into the Homes aged seven and often belted black and blue by the cottage mother. She used to make me stand in the kitchen on a stool in the dark in bare feet and I was very frightened of the scrabbling noises I heard in the dark and screamed and screamed. Another girl reported her and she was removed.

That was the only bad part of my time with Barnardo's. The new cottage mother said, 'You must be Enid', and smiled and I thought all my Christmasses had come at once.

71

I tried to come to Australia with my friends from 1934, but didn't quite pass my medical. In our year only 20 girls passed from the 50 entered. My friends wrote to me and they all liked it.
At last I was in an Australian party with Miss Hutchinson and Miss Edwards. I went to work straight away. My position was as nanny and assistant housekeeper to Sir Bertram Stevens, Premier after Jack Lang, where I was very happy.
Married while there, that's 58 years ago, I am very proud of my son and daughter and my five grand children, three of whom have completed university.

Dennis Downham
1936

I arrived on 3rd December 1936 in the *Otranto* on a lovely summer day. I spent four years at Mowbray Park Farm.

Me aged 11

Aged 15, I was sent onto a wheat and sheep farm at Gilgandra. I worked at a few farms and then returned to Sydney.

Many former Barnardo boys are now working farms on their own account; others are share farmers, and many have been in the same position from eight to ten years, advancing steadily during that time in usefulness to their employers and securing increasing pay for their exertions. One boy is a teacher in the Barker College, Hornsby. Two are in the Bush Brotherhood, and several in the police force.

I always remember a quote in the front of the Church of England Book of Common Prayer we each received on leaving the Home, dated 28th October, which Madame Rees wrote in 1940:

'And when the last great Scorer comes to write against your name, He'll ask not if you won or lost, but how you played the game'.

Madame Rees

My only regret is not ever knowing my real family and missing out on some of my early education.

A68 Mustang Fighter

I joined the RAAF where I finally qualified as a Fitter ll A. I spent time in Japan with the Occupation Force, (BCOF) at Iwakuni with 82 Squadron. On returning to Australia, I was allocated to five Mustang A68 fighter aircraft, which were deck cargo on a merchant ship to Australia from Japan. I took my discharge and was married - that was over 48 years ago! We settled in Melbourne where I worked in the commercial airline industry.

I'm very grateful to Dr Barnardo's Homes. At times we thought we were hard done by, but to control a mob of young lads, there had to be a certain amount of discipline and one of the secrets was to keep them occupied at all times, as the saying goes, 'idle hands get into mischief'. We were clothed, fed and fairly treated and I feel we were luckier than some of the 'outside kids' in some respects.

Harry completed his education at Barker College and then worked for GEC and Prudential, interrupted by over four years service in the AIF. He retired in 1986.

Harry Gerstle
1937

Harry Gerstle, a Townsville resident for the past 50 years, was German born. He says, 'Things did not look too rosy for people of a non-Aryan background. An invitation from an Australian relative was accepted with alacrity. I was 15, too young to travel alone, so my parents, learning that a group of Barnardo boys would be travelling in the *Otranto* in 1937, asked if the leaders would keep a watchful eye on me. I remember the friendliness and cheerfulness of the boys, but sadly have only kept in touch with one, Eric Leonard'.

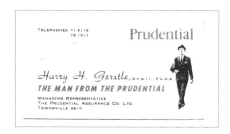

Harry was awarded the Medal of the Order of Australia in 1985 particularly for work with the Royal Queensland Bush Children's Health Scheme.

Ruby Penney
1937

I was seven years old when I came over. I don't remember being asked. My mother was single. Her fiance had gone to Canada and didn't even know about me.

I hated my first job as housekeeper to a spinster who went off to play bridge most evenings, leaving me alone. Her house was next to a church and it was too quiet. I ran away from there.

Then I went to work for the Reverend Allan Walker, notable in the Methodist Church, and his wife. He established 'Lifeline', a telephone counselling service for those in trouble. They were always lovely to me and unofficially adopted me. I have a Christmas card here signed 'from mum and dad' from them. I worked for them for many years.

I was happily married and have four boys, (one died in a biking accident), twelve grandchildren and four great-grandchildren. Unfortunately I was widowed.

Ruby, now Mrs Clee, and Ron live quietly at Werris Creek. They have a beautiful garden with vegetables and flowers all the year round. The house is full of Ruby's handiwork.

Coming out aged seven years ten months

I'm grateful to Barnardo's. We were better fed and clothed than a lot of people when we were in Barnardo's.

When I married Ron Clee, the Walkers gave us a beautiful wedding reception at their home.

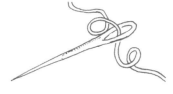

Christmas Party aboard the Otranto

Roger Slaughter
1937

I was born and baptised in 1927 in Slough, and admitted by my mother. She had been fostered as a child, and was in service, living with a great-aunt in Berkshire, when she became pregnant with me. The putative father disappeared and could not be traced as he had given a false name. My mother kept me with her at a Day Servant's Hostel in Chelsea for over a year. Three years later she became pregnant again, the father denying responsibility. I have never met this child, my brother. Unsuccessful efforts were made to trace my mother when arrangements were being made for me to emigrate. She had been working at a school and supposedly left to get married. That was 1934 and she disappeared from my life for ever.

Looking through my school progress reports from Mowbray Park Farm School, I remember the battle of wills I had with those in charge as I read the comments: reserved, deep, determined, stubborn, a high order of intelligence, a keen analytical mind, moody, 'plays to the gallery', wayward moods, inclined to be stubborn, temperamental, adopts an air of superiority with other boys. Roly Paxton, the Farm Manager and I had a love/hate relationship.

He wrote of me,'...considers himself rather superior to farm work' and '...not fond of hard work for which he has a supercilious disdain'.

A fragment from a letter to me from Matron Ethel Rathbone in 1952, signed 'your sincere friend'.
She would reason with me about my behaviour - as always a wonderful, patient, intelligent friend

I was in my sixties when my late wife secretly contacted Barnardo's After Care, and I learned of my early childhood from a sheaf of papers pulled from an envelope in the mail. I thanked her sincerely, but the information threw me into turmoil. Having been strong in all parts of my life, both for myself and others, I felt suddenly vulnerable. What was I supposed to do with these bits of information that had come so late?

Roger talking with Ann Howard

Lining up for a drink at Barnardo's Boy's School in England

On leaving Mowbray Park Farm School, I was contented with the positions found for me, having a room to myself and being treated like one of the family. I worked hard, neither drank nor gambled, and learned a lot about cattle. I read books, played cards with my employers and ate my meals with them. I was in a rich pasture area where the farmers made a good living. I remained in the area all my life, had a happy marriage and brought up my family here. I am now semi-retired with an extensive garden full of azaleas, camellias and rare and unusual trees, occasionally open to the public.

83

Peter Chaffey
1937

Peter and Reginald Chaffey

Reginald Chaffey came out in 1937, in the *Otranto,* but his brother Peter had to stay in Boys Garden City, Essex, because of illness. He was very disappointed but the masters, Mr Du Prau and Mr Appleton said that he would go to Australia the following year. This did not happen because of the war looming.

Reginald settled happily at Mowbray Park Farm but one day in 1938 became ill. All the boys were looking forward to the Picton Show and so he kept quiet . At the show, the little snowy-haired and fair-skinned boy collapsed and was taken to Camden Hospital with diphtheria, where he died shortly afterwards. His brother, Peter was told that he died coming out in the *Otranto.*

For sixty years, Peter wondered about the true nature of his brother's death, until his friend Debbie, after watching *Lost Children of the Empire,* urged him to seek information from the Child Migrant Trust.

In 1997, Eric Leonard, Bill Webber, Ken Church and Ted Burns were leaving for a reunion of the 1937 party in the UK and were anxious to trace Peter and tell him of the sad circumstances of his brother's death. We traced him through the Child Migrant's Trust with the help of Bill Hoyles. Peter put some money in Eric's hands and asked him to

place some flowers on his brother's grave at Camden. They found three other Barnardo boy's graves nearby: Tommy Dear of the 1936 party, Robert Griggs of the 1934 party and William Vincent of the 1939 party. Eric sent a photograph back of Bill Webber, Ken Church and himself by the grave with the flowers.

Peter was overjoyed to later find through the Salvation Army, two half brothers, living in Herne Bay and one in Ashford, Kent. Peter's father married again after his mother's death.

The gravestone reads: In affectionate memory of Reginald George Chaffey of the Barnardo Farm School Picton Died 23-3-38 Aged 10 years

Aged 74, I look back with adult thoughts that what was done for me was with the best of intentions. But very bewildering when you are taken from all you know. It seems strange that I have three children of my own, eight grandchildren and seven great-grandchildren.

Marjorie Marchant

1937

My birth mother had been seduced by her father, which was kept secret. She was 16 when she had me in a London unmarried mother's hospital. My grandmother, kept me for two years. I was given to a Mr and Mrs Fenwick who were childless but wanted to adopt me. Up to twelve, I was Marjorie Fenwick, then the lady I called Mum died, and my foster father remarried.

Old enough at 12 or 13 years to know my life, suddenly all that you know, people who you think are 'mum' and 'dad', turn out not to be. Suddenly you are told your name is not your real name and given another - mine was 'Bicker' and the girls were horrible, (said it meant quarrelsome). How I hated it.

The new 'stepmother' knew that I was not legally adopted, so my father put me in the Girl's Village Home. When I went for selection to Australia, hardly knowing where it was on the map, I was happy. After the medical tests I realised I would never see my 'Dad' again. I wrote asking if he could stop me going. An awful shock awaited me at the Governor's Office . I was asked why I didn't want to go and called 'a most ungrateful child', my clothes and everything they was ready. I had to write to Mr Fenwick and say I was most anxious to go, asking for his blessing in my own writing and spelling. Two weeks before we sailed he visited me at Barkingside. As 'I wanted to go', he'd signed. Before he left me for the last time, as I thought, he said, 'I can't stop you going, be a good girl, when you are

21 and of age, if you want to come back, if you only save two pennies for the fare, I will help you'.

When I was demobbed, I went to the Orient Shipping Company to book a passage. The clerk said, 'Yes, madame, when would you like a passage'. 'In a year's time'. I knew the staff at work would not be pleased. I told 'dad' but not my 'stepmother' as I knew she had a son and I would be an intruder from the past. I saved hard at a job in a Katoomba hotel, where I was very happy. The staff tried to persuade me to stay another year, as England was still very much rationed, but I was 21.

I found my birth mother in 1969. I was lucky she wanted to see me but of course there was no bonding. She won't correspond with me because she has an adopted son, who doesn't know what my true relationship is to her. Which is really sad because he has the love of a mother who is really mine.

On December 28th 1946 I married a young man who had gone through the war years in the AIF. It was a hard life as

we hit the 1946-7 winter. He was a cowman. He worked hard for £1 per week and a cottage. We were married for 49 years and eight months, almost our golden wedding, when he died.

85

Eric Leonard

Me on admission to Barnardo's

I was born on August 22nd, 1926 and three years later I was placed in the care of Susanna and William Egmore by Rose Leonard at Swannington, Norwich, Norfolk as Derrick Egmore. Apparently I arrived in a chauffeur driven car which would have raised a few eyebrows in their small village. I have dim memories during my next five years, of carrying a milk can, of feeling happy in a warm kitchen, of playing with gypsy children and their horses and seeing the patches in the snow after they left at about 4 am in the mornings.

My great-grandmother, Fred Egmore, my father in the middle of the back row, and granny Egmore with eight of her eleven children

Gran and grandad Egmore with gran's sister Ettie on the left

The only photograph I have of my father, Fred Egmore as an adult with an aunt and her child given to me May 1999

[handwritten text at top of page, partially legible:]
...illegitimate deserted child of unknown paternity. The mother Rose Leonard
...is known about her. In Aug 1929 she placed Eric in the care of h~
husband William (over 70) and they have ever since maintained him
...ce of the mother has been lost. The case illustrates how easy it is in the
...a child. Eric is bright and healthy; during the past five years he has...
...foster parents address is 'near the Post Office, Swannington near ?
Norwich'.
                                                        Full A~t by foster mother

The above admission statement by The Rev W~reads:
Illegitimate and deserted child of unknown paternity. The mother Rose
Leonard was a domestic servant: nothing else is known about her. On
August 1929, she placed Eric in the care of Mrs Susanna Egmore (70)
and her husband William (over 70) and they have since maintained him
for the past five years and all trace of the mother has been lost. The
case illustrates how easy it is in the present state of the law to get rid
of a child. Eric is bright and healthy; during the past five years he has
had no medical attention whatsoever.

On 9th August 1934 I was placed in Barnardo's Homes. A matron
took me and Alec Topling by the hand and sat us down side by side at
a desk. 'Alec Topling and Derek Egmore, you are now to be John
Franklin and Eric John Leonard. Write it out twenty times and don't
forget it'. We looked at each other and did what she said.

ERIC JOHN LEONARD

Admitted—8th August, 1934.   Age—7 years, 11 months.
Born—22nd August, 1926, at 103, St Dunstans Road, Pulham.
Religion of mother not known.
If Baptized—not known.
Full Agreement—signed by Susanna Egmore (as guardian).

Path —Boy illegitimate (see below).
Mother—Rose Leonard, was domestic servant: address at time of Eric's birth =
189, Stephendale Road, Pulham, whereabouts unknown for last five years.

    Application by Rev. J. D. Wortley, Swannington Rectory, Norwich, who
supplied particulars.
    Deserted child.
    The mother was a domestic servant; nothing else is known about her. In
Aug 1929, she placed Eric in the care of Mrs. Susanna Egmore (70) and her
husband William (over 70), and they have ever since maintained him, and for the
past five years all trace of the mother has been lost.
    Eric is bright and healthy; during the past five years he has had no medical
attention whatever. The last consecutive six months were spent c/o Mr. Egmore,
Swannington, Norwich, Norfolk.

    Relatives :—

Putative father:— — whereabouts unknown.
Foster parents—Mr. & Mrs. Egmore, nr. Post Office Swannington, Norwich.

Although my first eight years of life are a blank, I remember being taken into a Barnardo's home one night and fitted with an oversize nightshirt. I remember the matron's cold hand leading me to a large dormitory. I remember saying my prayers through sobs and sneaking a look at fifty or so other boys like myself.

I need to remember and know, it's important to know, it's my birthright, and my right to have this knowledge to pass on to my children and grand-children.

My boarding out photo

A typical dormitory

Happy days

I was only at Stepney Causeway a couple of weeks when on 29th August 1937 I was sent to Isleham, Cambridgeshire to be fostered out to Peter and Ann Beckett. I went up on the train with a tall, skinny woman in a grey suit. I was one of three boys fostered by these lovely people. A lot of boys were sent up to this area because it was close to the trains. I am still friendly with Henry Gawthorpe who was also fostered out in Isleham. Many went on to the Watts Naval Training College at Norfolk. I shared a room with Donald Beckett and was very happy there. Their eldest daughet Pamela would soon leave school to go into service. I really missed her.

Mrs Beckett used to boil onion pudding made from Mr Beckett's onions from his allotment. He supplied fresh vegetables and we used to pick watercress from a sparkling creek. We had earth toilets with wooden seats outside and one of the household tasks was to dig a hole for night soil. Some people threw lime down the hole. Our house was one of four and Mrs Fuller at the end was well known to all the others. She was a large noisy lady. If he went up to the Comrades Club to have a drink, Dad would bring back a bar of 5 Boys chocolate to share. I used to go boxing at Bert Brown's barn and Donald wanted to come with me and used to cry when he could not because he was too young. The villagers would be twitching the curtains when the Barnardo's inspector came every six months to check on me. She brought her own scales and hung them in the doorway, came upstairs and pulled the bedclothes back and asked me if I was happy.

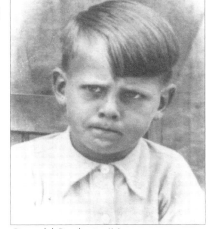

Donald Beckett: 'Your new brother is coming tomorrow, my mother said and here was Eric, seven years and ten months old wearing short trousers, a jumper and a striped tie and carrying a bag with a drawstring. I was four and my sister was twelve...'

The villagers were accepting and I don't remember any problems with them but some of the teachers were a bit terse. One teacher gave me a backhander and I remember falling against the partition making such a noise my dignity was injured. I received another whack when I stood up. I took an instant dislike to all the male teachers who bullied us 'Home' boys as we were known in the village. When I told Mrs Beckett, she put her hat on and went straight down to the school and told the teacher, 'any belting and I'll do it'.

Miss Watson, another teacher was beautiful and caring and I used to rush down to school to take her books from the cane basket on her bicycle and carry them in for her. We kids had little gangs: 'The Pits', the 'The Eastenders', 'The Back Row' and 'Maltings Lane '.

Donald in Mr Beckett's arms, Mrs Beckett and me

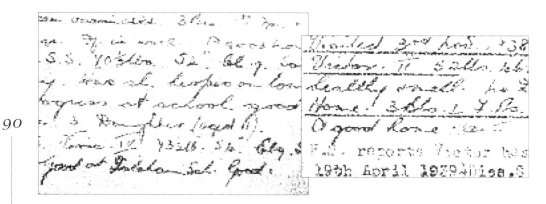

Barnardo's Inspector Reports.
Under 'In strictest confidence' the inspector notes that a teacher was removed from the school 'because of indiscretions' and that I was one of the boys concerned. Throughout the reports is the word 'good' - good boy, good home, good at school - but they still took me away. One family outing was to an an aunt Jane's. She was all dressed in black. Donald and I had to sit on two boxes either side of the fire and only speak if we were spoken to. The adults would drink wheat wine and talk around the table as the evening got darker and darker and we wriggled on our boxes. Sometimes we would be given lemonade.

Mr Beckett followed his father as a bargeman carrying coals on the canals and we all went weeding and fruit-picking for the nearby farmers. I was so happy that I thought I'd be there for ever and ever but three years later I was asked by my foster father to choose between Australia, Canada or the Navy. Some of my friends chose the Navy and went down with the *Hood*. I chose Australia, not knowing anything about it at all, but I wanted to stay with these good people, I thought I'd stay with them for ever. They in turn never forgot me.

July 21st 1937, feeling upset and bewildered, I was returned to Boys Garden City, Essex. Why? Why was I suddenly taken away from my dad, mother and caring sister and a happy little brother. This question was not answered until my 71st year. When I was eleven, I became one of 'the Australian boys' as Captain Rees called us.

We were taken to Australia House in London. We got the impression Australia was a vast, sun-drenched country where we would ride ponies. To prepare us for migration, we slept out in tents on the outskirts of Woodford Bridge. One little kid was frightened of the dark and didn't want to go out to the latrines. The other boys were quick to notice and would scare him by lighting up the inside of their mouth by torchlight and making noises. If you wet the bed, you couldn't go overseas, so he used to get in someone else's bed and wet it. He never made it to Australia.

There were lots of tests, eye, teeth, hearing examinations, weight, height, IQ, and we learned to swim. It was better if you had mumps and measles and didn't have flat feet or anaemia. They didn't take anyone wearing glasses or who was colour blind to Australia.

We went to Barnardo's Garden City and were issued with khaki uniforms and Panama hats for the voyage, which we used to spin across the grass or sail on the river when unobserved. As the days grew colder, the 'Australian Boys' were sent to Bognor Regis, Sussex for a month, possibly for the bracing air. Life-long bonds were formed among the boys then. We were told they only wanted the best for Australia. We visited Australia House and were shown pictures of the ponies we would ride to school.

We berthed at Pyrmont and we were loaded into a truck with seats made of boxes. Off we went to Mowbray Park Farm School. We had arrived. I learned fast at Mowbray Park, Picton in the southern highlands of NSW, 50 miles out of Sydney.
W B Ladd, ex-Army, who had been gassed in the First World War, had a belt ready if you gave him cheek, but he was fair and just and you knew where you were with him. Captain Rees was ex-Navy and also strict but fair.

The 1937 party on board the Otranto on arrival
l to r: front row: Alan Moore Reginald Chaffey, Norman Jones, Eric Cummins
Kenneth Church Second row: Raymond Lusher Ernest Sharpling Ted Burns Denis
Underwood Bill Sinden Ernest Hayward Third row: Terence Cox Richard Warriner
John Franklin Arthur Hook John Bown George Symons Norman Smith. Back row:
Fred Small -Ronald Baker - Peter Butler Roger Slaughter

They both had control of the party coming out from Tilbury. As a trainee at the Farm Training School, I learning to milk and worked in the stables and yards and had general duties like cutting wood and caring for poultry. My friend, Tom D'Arcy was a very good axeman. We supplied Mowbray Park and Burwood, the Girl's Home, with milk, butter and eggs and chickens to roast at Easter and Christmas. I loved the mould board plough with one horse pulling the heavy plough and one horse steering a straight furrow.

  I followed, pushing down, with clouds of dust, willy wagtails, crows fluttering behind. I'd stop and give the horses oats at midday and then go on until sundown. I also loved stump grubbing and splitting logs with an adze. We were trained thoroughly and some Barnardo's boys are still farmers.

Eric at the top, branding a calf with Gerald Vincent holding the leg and Eric Metherell

As a schoolboy, we were given 2d a week out of which we banked 1d and spent 1d at the tuckshop. Leaving school as a trainee we got 6d a week, after three months 1s and after 6 months 1s..6d. If you got a good report card, you were allowed to go to Picton or Thirlmere to the Saturday matinee. Before leaving, we would sit in the shade of a big tree, oiling our red farm boots with linseed oil, we'd discuss the latest film.

We sometimes cadged a lift for the five miles but it was quicker to run across the paddocks. You worked to a roster, which was placed on the notice board. Sport was a must for each boy. We had three teams: Wallabies, Kangaroos and Springboks.. The best day of my life was when I wore my farm boots to school for the last day as was the custom. The girls stayed until they were 14, going on to Burwood to learn domestic duties.

Looking back, we had a good life, but although well-treated, I felt a prisoner within the boundaries of Mowbray Park. The schoolteacher, a big, happy Australian kept telling us how lucky we were to be in Australia.

One day, when I was in charge of the dairy, a big bloke came into my room before the afternoon milking and berated me about the state of my room. I said, 'It's nothing to do with you' and he hit me hard under the ear. I crashed into the wall and fell on the floor. Two of my mates ran up, one throwing me a cricket stump. I hit my aggressor hard across the knees and as he fell,I told my mates, 'I'm out of here'. I went to Thirlmere and my mates brought my clothes over.   It was known as 'doing a bunk'. I went to the Ashtons, a local family I knew. Mrs Ashton gave me a room and I found a job at Smith Sons and Rees at Redfern making spark plugs for planes.

I put my age up and tried to join the Navy. Mr Ladd said, 'Why didn't you ask me, you could have joined at a younger age if your guardian, (Barnardo's) agreed'. Manpower, the authority of the day, it was wartime, said I had to go to the land. At this time, my foster mother was still enquiring after me as this letter shows:

93

A lady in the home who was a donor to Barnardo's wanted to adopt the youngest boy, (Robert McCaughan). She lived in Queensland and normally I wouldn't have been allowed over the border unless I was in the armed forces, but I was sent to Blackall in Queensland, to work on her sheep station in October 1943.

The lovable and caring Miss Moore, took me to buy a new three-piece suit and by 4pm I was on Central station with steam trains snorting, whistles blowing, service people hurrying about and the smell of soot which has always stayed with me. I seemed to be the only civilian. My destination would be 60 miles from the nearest town. I was sent to Blackall on a train like a piece of luggage with a big ticket tied to my lapel and a suitcase, with my name and destination. 'Eric, don't you get off this train until you get to Blackall!' said Miss Moore. Barnardos were sending me to Queensland but I had to report to them until I was twenty-one. I was 17 years old, going to a sheep and cattle station in a new three-piece suit. I took off my label as soon as Miss Moore, waving to the train, was out of sight. Servicemen were asleep on the floor and up on the luggage racks. The whole trip took three days. When I got to Roma Street, Brisbane, I bought some custard apples and mangoes and sat on the platform most of the day, not daring to leave, Miss Moore's words ringing in my ears. The train went all night to Rockhampton and then I had to change to a day train to Jericho, where I talked to the train drover, (the train was carrying sheep and cattle).

94

I finally arrived at my destination Saturday evening. Mrs Bows, the licensee put me on the verandah of the Barcoo Hotelwhere I had the first taste and smell of outback Queensland. On the barcoo River - oh! the smell of bore water - which I was able to catch up with again - during my return to Blackall, after 50 years, nothing had changed other than the licensee.

When my new employer arrived Sunday morning 9 am, he looked me up and down and said: 'Are you ready?' We drove till 3 pm to his station and I opened about ten different sets of gates. His words rang in my ears, 'God Almighty, the first thing you've got to learn is to open and shut a pair of gates'.

About 3 pm and he showed me a bunk on the back verandah with a green mosquito net over it. There was a wardrobe next to it full of dust.

'Change your clothes and come and have a cup of tea. Can you hear those bells? They are the cows you will need to find and milk in the morning - plus the night horse. We will be up at 5 am to go mustering - hope they taught you to ride at the Farm School. There has been a dust storm - you will have to get used to this country'.

The station was 23 000 acres, carrying 12 000 cross bred-sheep, 200 head of cattle and 50 horses. It was 100 kms to Blackall where we got our supplies. The employer was ex-army and he did it hard, especially in droughts. On arrival, I worked 80 hours a week for seventy five cents and my keep and my employer treated me like a second-class citizen. I didn't complain. I thought I was lucky to have a job.

My employer had three sons. Their second son, a pilot, was shot down in WWII and kept alive for three months by the 'fuzzy-wuzzy angels' in New Britain. The eldest son was in the Air Force, serving in the Middle East, the youngest one was at boarding school. That left the boss and me and sometimes his wife when it wasn't too hot. At 5am, he would wake me by running his stick along the corrugated iron wall above my bed, 'Get up and make the fire and put the kettle on!'.

After a bit I moved into the shearer's shed and when we went into town I bought a Technico battery and wired up a big old wireless - company at last. The boss had a a charcoal cool safe with wet hessian and watr bags. Electricity was rationed because we had a generator. When the young son came home for holidays,he used to wear white jodhpurs, which I had to wash getting rid of horse and sheep grease. They grew grapes and had a nice garden, but water was always a problem. It wasn't good land, there was just a lot of it, desert country.

While mustering, the three dogs would get bindis in their paws and one black and white collie would jump up on my saddle and hold up his paws for me to pull the bindis out. This collie soon became my real friend. Oh, how I missed the company of the farm school. In the six months I worked the property, I only went to town twice. The youngest son was taking the T-Ford to tennis on the Sunday which was my day off. I suggested to my employer that he pick up the mail from Enniskillen and he refused roughly.

4th September, 1944.

Dear Mr. Ladd,

Eric John Leonard. N.S.W.11/37.

In reply to your enquiry for some information regarding the relatives of the above-named, we have looked up our records and I give the following information.

Eric John Leonard was admitted to these Homes on the 9th August, 1934 when he was nearly 8 years old. He was born on the 22nd August, 1926 at Fulham. Eric's mother's name was Rose Leonard, a domestic servant and at the time of Eric's birth she was living in Fulham. When Eric was quite a baby she put him in the care of Mrs. Susanna Egmore of Swannington, Norwich, who with her husband, continued to maintain him until he was admitted to our care as mentioned above. Mr. and Mrs. Egmore were said to be very fond of the boy and the last enquiry we received from Mrs. Egmore was in February, 1938 from Swannington, Nr. Norwich, Norfolk. Eric was later boarded out under our care, and our foster-mother, who also states she was very fond of Eric, wrote as recently as August last. Her address is Mrs. F. Beckett, 4, Back Road, Isleham, Nr. Ely, Cambs.

I trust the above information will enable you to satisfy Eric's enquiry. We have no information whatever about Eric's father and we have never heard from the mother, and have no idea where she now is.

I decided there and then to leave, on my next visit to Blackall, but how? I worked as a cowboy at Blackall for six months on a model property, 'Duneria'. This employer respected my expertise with horses and dairy cattle. He lent me a book, *Try Anything Once*, and advised me to have a good look around Queensland. I went into the shearing sheds again and thanks to Barnardo training I was twice seconded to the kitcchen as the shearer's cook.

1945 was the year of the Shearer's Strike and it was difficult to get work in Queensland. Two pals and I travelled to the coast of north Queensland obtaining contract to cut sugar cane. Whilst really hard work, I enjoyed the money earned. At Barnardo's we'd been told 'you're an Ozzie now', but I felt I could make my own decisions. I'd been sending food parcels, to my foster parents, Mr and Mrs Beckett and wanted to see them. It was actually about this time that I lost contact with them.

I had been at Bannockburn for over nine months. In June I headed back to Sydney for Founder's Day, hungry for news of my 'family'. The boss's wife took me to lunch at a restaurant where the squatters ate. I had lamb and caper sauce. After the first mouthful, I looked up at her and said, 'Whoever killed this sheep did a terrible job!' I flew to Sydney in a Douglas - it took all day. I picked up a mail order suit and got talking to the sales assistant. He offered me boarding with his mother. They were racehorse trainers at Randwick.

I asked the tram driver where the police recruitment centre was because the sergeant at Hughenden, north-west Queensland had advised me to join the Northern Territory Mounted police. I enjoyed the bush, riding, and knew I got on well with aboriginal stockmen. I stepped off the tram into a new future - or so I thought.

'Can you ride a horse?'

'I think so', I replied.

They put me on a horse then sent me down to Circular Quay for a medical. While I waited to see the recruiting officer, I stared at the photographs on the wall and realised I was in the wrong place.

'Where's the Northern Territory Mounted Police Recruiting?'

'Why? We've got Mounted Police down here'.

'I want to go to the country'

'You'll go to the country all right, son. And you'll be a policeman too, just don't let us down', stated the sergeant.

I passed the medical and the entrance exam and then the officer asked me for my birth certificate. I felt my cheeks burning as I told him I didn't have one although in those days, it was not uncommon as there were many itinerants. Mr Ladd sent away for one for me. When my birth certificate finally arrived, I stared down at my mother's name: Rose Leonard. I was twenty years old before I knew my mother's name.

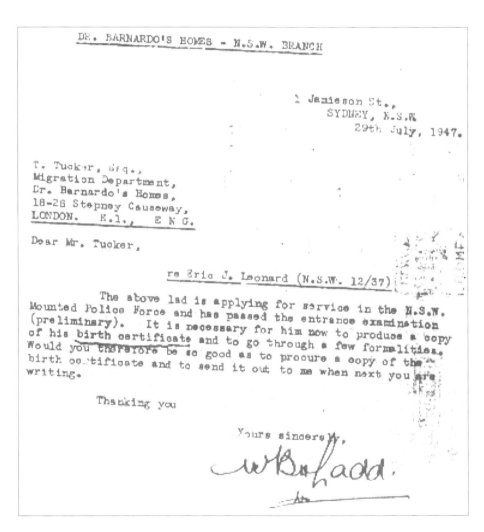

This young man is typical of many who have taken advantage of the present opportunities for branching out into careers, or trades. He came to Australia at the age of eleven, and, after training at the Farm School, spent a number of years on the land, which helped to fit him for his chosen career—a member of the Mounted Police Force.

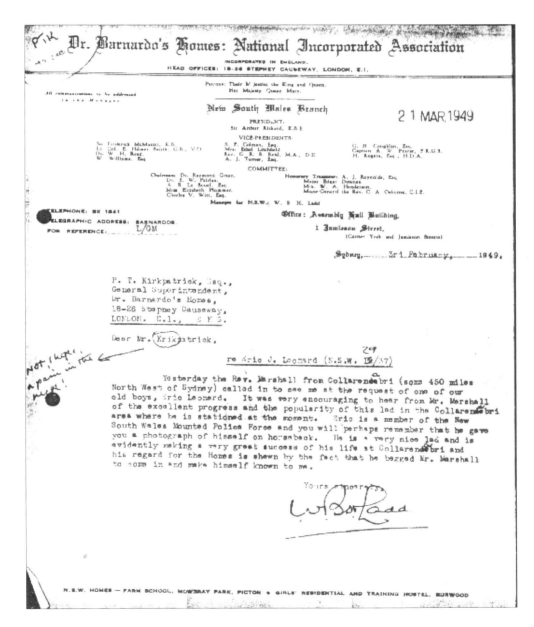

P. T. Kirkpatrick, Esq.,
General Superintendent,
Dr. Barnardo's Homes,
18-26 Stepney Causeway,
LONDON. E.1., E N G.

Dear Mr. Kirkpatrick,

re Eric J. Leonard (N.S.W. 19/37)

Yesterday the Rev. Marshall from Collarenebri (some 450 miles North West of Sydney) called in to see me at the request of one of our old boys, Eric Leonard. It was very encouraging to hear from Mr. Marshall of the excellent progress and the popularity of this lad in the Collarenebri area where he is stationed at the moment. Eric is a member of the New South Wales Mounted Police Force and you will perhaps remember that he gave you a photograph of himself on horseback. He is a very nice lad and is evidently making a very great success of his life at Collarenebri and his regard for the Homes is shewn by the fact that he begged Mr. Marshall to come in and make himself known to me.

Yours sincerely,

W. B. H. Ladd

*Not (hope!)
again in the
neck!*

The bonding in the NSW PoliceForce is as strong as that of Barnardos. I was used to being disciplined and liked a structured life. I shall always be grateful for the education I received from them.

Dr. Barnardo's Homes

National Incorporated Association

INCORPORATED IN ENGLAND

New South Wales Branch

PHONE: B X 1841

Office: Assembly Hall Building,
1 Jamieson Street,

Sydney, May 12th 1952

Dear Mr. Lucette

Eric Leonard NSW 29 (1937)

This Old Boy is in the N.S.W. Police + is hoping shortly to be put regularly on plain clothes duty. He has had a successful try-out!

He is anxious to know something of his back ground (with matrimonial intentions, I suspect!) Could I have a copy of his history sheet by air mail please.

Yours sincerely

P. T. Kirkpatrick

100

General Superintendent's Office.	TO	Migration Department.

OUR REF. EHL/EM   30.10.58.

re Eric Leonard (NSW 1937)

I would suggest you write to Mr. Charles as follows:-

"Here is the file of Eric Leonard who, so far as I can see, was admitted under that name. The foster parents were nearly 80 in 1943. It hardly seems worthwhile expecting to find them now. Would you kindly return the file when you have read it?"

General Superintendent.

the Million Dollar Round Table at Atlanta. To qualify for membership, one had to hav sold A$1 000 000 in one calendar year and have regard from one's peers. I was by this time a six-year MDRT qualifier and I recounted my personal experience of being reared in an orphanage to underscore the value and importance of serving the family market. 'You may ask why after spending my younger years in an institution, I feel qualified to talk to you about family selling'. The answer is obvious. 'The need I feel to provide for the security of the family unit', I said. 'The desire and envy that one feels looking in from the outside at people who are nurtured in the bosom of family life cfeates a need and desire for this family life far greater than is likely to be felt by one who takes family life for granted'.

I joined Mercantile Mutual Life as a life agent in January 1980.
I have enjoyed a fruitful working partnerhip with Mercantile Mutual Life since and made many friends.

I feel child migrants must look back and be proud of the contribution they have made and the lifestyles they have achieved. Ella Wheeler Wilcox wrote, 'Tis the set of a soul that decides its goal and not the calm or the strife'.

When Donald Beckett, his foster brother, visited Eric in Sydney in February 1999, they laughed together about the old times. Then Donald grew sad. 'One day, a woman in a grey suit came and told mum to get Eric's things ready because they were coming to get him', Donald mused. 'It was terrible, mum didn't want him to go'.

Eric goes west

Sports Day 1937

At the Barnardo Farm School Annual Sports Day in 1937, 100 boys took part in front of throngs of visitors. Twenty three events took place between 1pm and 4 pm. Laughter rang in the sunshine at the greasy pig contest and comic boxing match. Many prizes were presented by E W Fairfax, Chairman of the Executive Committee of Dr Barnardo's Homes. Captain R D Rees was boxing referee and judge, Mr Heath, Farm Manager was Master of Ceremonies. Mr Firth, the Headmaster was starter, with Mr Tucker as assistant starter. First judge was Mr Unwin, Farm Foreman, second judge Mr Rhodes. Carpentry Instructor, third judge Mr Griffiths, Bootmaker, and recorder of results, Mr Cornwell, Sportsmaster assisted by Mr Bowden.

Among the many winners were Dermott Reilly who won a watch for heavyweight boxing, Ossie Davies who won a prize for 'best all round and most useful boy', Eric Dodge, the 'best trainee' and Eric Barrat and Norman Bartlett who won pocket knives for the two best-behaved boys on the voyage out to Australia in the *Otranto*.

His weakness gives him **STRENGTH**

Over 70 Barnardo Boys and Girls from all parts of NSW celebrated Founder's Day on Monday June 27, 1938 at the Farm School. From over 200 000 children admitted to Dr Barnardo's Homes in the UK, about 2 000 had arrived in Australia as child migrants to be trained for domestic and farm work.

107

Among questions asked in the Senate on the 14th November 1934 was that from Senator Collins asking the Minister representing the Prime Minister: 1. Is it a fact that (a) The Barnardo's Homes Society of London is despatching a contingent of British youths to Australia (b) that the arrivals, both girls and boys are now in Sydney 2. If so, does he consider that immigration should be allowed to continue in view of the fact that tens of thousands of young Australians are reported to be unable to secure employmemt of any kind.

In 1939, the Farm School won 23 first and nine second places at the Picton Show for their produce. The *Sydney Morning Herald* quoted, 'Pupils of the school are eagerly sought by employers and it is anticipated that the great majority of them will enter a life of prosperity and usefulness'.

I was born north of Belfast. Mother and father both died and the family was split up. Father was a hawker. I was the youngest of five. The two eldest went to Fairbridge in 1934 and the other three were sent to Stepney Causeway. We were fostered out together to very nice people. It was the early 1940's.

Robert McCaughan
1939

Harry at the top, then Jon, me, and Tom with George in front. Being with my brothers helped, but they used to torment me with big blue-tongue lizards

The two eldest were both in the Army and one of them eventually tracked me down. I never saw Tom until I was 48 years old. I was six when they told me I was going to ride horses to school, but it was always a bus!

Once I lost my shoes and they made me wear girl's shoes for a week and called me Rosie.

I ran away from the Home when Roly Paxton was there in 1945 to 1946, when there were only about six of us left.

George ran away and they got him digging around the Home and he ran away again so they sent him to Gosford. I didn't see him for 15 years. I had a bit of a bike made from bits I found and I cleared off and found a job with a charcoal burner, (there was no petrol then) a few miles from the Home. I used to take the veggies up on Saturdays from the Home to old Mr Walker, living next door to Harry Smith.

We got friendly and he employed me. After Harry couldn't afford to pay me, I went to work for the egg man. I got my driving licence and settled in Thirlmere. After the egg contract finished, I worked for Picton Council. That was a happy time, Australia was a quieter place. We used to walk four or five miles to a dance and no-one ever bothered us. I married a girl in Bankstown and worked at Cabramatta.

I was an ambulance driver, bus driver for 15 years and then a truckie for Taubmans. I'm still driving a fork lift for them aged 68. I think hard work is the secret of a happy life.

If Barnardo's hadn't looked after us, we wouldn't be here now.

Strathaird

I would like to tell you boys at home, a little about the activities of your brothers out here. There are at present, ninety-six here, from various branches in England, seventy are attending the Barnardo School and the remaining twenty six, who are fourteen years, have left School, and are under a year's course of training in the different parts of the farm, before leaving for situations.

Our farm is one of one hundred and sixty acres, situated in one of the most beautiful and healthy positions in New South Wales, and the course of training covers instruction in general farming, ploughing, mowng, cultivating, fertilising, fencing, etc., milking cows and general dairy work, attending to pigs horses, felling trees to provide firewood. The boys receive instruction in the growing of crops: maize, sorghum, and potatoes, mangolds, pumpkins, melons etc

In the poultry section we have about a hundred chickens of all ages, from the tiny little incubator chicks to the grim old roosters, and the laying hens give us about one hundred eggs every day so you see that we can milk the cows for them to have fresh milk to drink, while the hens lay fresh eggs for them to eat. Another favourite part of the training is orchards, and the growing of apples, pears, quinces, lemons, oranges, tangerines and tomatoes.

The boys are also instructed in house and laundry, and the course is completed by a month's instruction in carpentry and boot repairing. Agricultural lectures are given on one evening a week.

117

Both Rugby and Soccer, Cricket and Tennis sides have an excellent record this year, not only for winning matches, but for clean, sports like play, and fixtures are eagerly sought by the other teams in the district.

Trainees and schoolboys have plenty of fun with picnics, camp fire nights, etc., occasionally plenty of excitement, when bushfires break out on neighbouring farms, and our boys, who are great fire-fighters, are called upon to help them out, each boy with a wetted sack. The creek through the estate is dammed and provides a splendid swimming pool, and provides a great deal of interest in the catching of tortoises and eels, whilst amongst other pets are baby opossums and lizards. Thousands of parrots fly around, and their plumage is so very beautiful, that the boys cannot resist the temptation of catching them for pets.

Stepney Causeway

Stepney Causeway proudly purchased, remains in the memory of the migrant children who passed through as a gloomy and frightening place, with trains rumbling mysteriously at night. Ninety years after the first home opened, Barnardo's moved to Barkingside and the old buildings were demolished

The opening of the Millions Club cottage for the 'Millionaires'

The opening of the Millions Club cottage at Mowbray Park Farm on July 15th, 1939. For 30 years, the remarkable old property Mowbray Park would be home to about 80 boys, from the age of seven with a minimum IQ of 92, who went to school and were taught to farm. One old boy, strolling around the 22 acres remembers the laughter as well as the tears, 'Those five years at Picton were among the happiest in my life. After a sea voyage half way around the world the eight kilometre stretch from Picton township to Mowbray Park was one of

the longest in my life and it took me a while to get used to the dryness of the landscape after England's green land, but I soon revelled in the wide open spaces and long summers. My memories of childhood are filled with running barefoot, swimming nude in the creek, catching turtles, stealing birds' eggs and chasing rabbits with our motley collection of dogs'.

119

"For God and Country"

THE ANNUAL REPORT

of

Dr. Barnardo's Homes

National Incorporated Association

(NEW SOUTH WALES BRANCH)

FOR THE YEAR
1939

World War II, generally considered to begin with German invasion of Poland on September 1 1939 meant Robert Menzies taking Australia to war. At the end of the 30's, the government was prepared to spend 43 million pounds on revitalising the Army. Most men who left for overseas were tradesmen and labourers and women stepped into their roles, battling high prices and lack of supplies. There would soon be a new category of orphans - war orphans. In the first three months of war, about 2 000 Barnardo boys 'answered the Empire's call'. In NSW 35 young Barnardo's men joined the AIF, RAAF and RAN, with ten serving in militia units. Many made wills in favour of the Homes before going into action.

In the sunfilled days at Mowbray Park Farm war seemed far away as the children's laughter echoed in through the old pines.

Mowbray Park House was built in classical Victorian style in1884 by an architect from England. For 30 of its 171 years, it would be a farm school for British child migrants.

CONCERT

PRESENTED BY THE GIRLS AND BOYS OF
DR. BARNARDO'S HOMES, PICTON.
In aid of
CAMDEN DISTRICT HOSPITAL
(CHILDREN'S WARD).
Town Hall, Camden,
Thursday, 18th May, 1939,
At 8 p.m.

PROGRAMME

1 —OPENING CHORUS, "It's a Grand Old World."
2 —A PERSIAN FANTASY, "Abou Hassan."
3 —SONG "I Love to Whistle."
4 —PLAY, "A Garden of Eden."
5 —SONG AND DANCE "Does Your Mother Come from Ireland," and TAP DANCING CHORUS, "The Fleet's in Port Again."

INTERVAL.

6. SONG, "Come Over on the Sunny Side."
7. SKETCH, "Paddy and the Ghost."
8.— COUNTRY DANCES, "Rufty Tufty," and "Gathering Peascods."
9.— PLAY, "The Grand Cham's Diamond."
10. SONG, "You've got to Smile when you say Goodbye."
11 —CLOSING CHORUS, "Aloha Oe."
THE NATIONAL ANTHEM

121

No further child migrant parties

The Second World War began touching children's lives after the Munich crisis of September 1938, when 150 refugee children arrived from western Europe in London. Within three days of declaration of war, on Sunday 3 September 1939 at 11 am, 2 500 Barnardo's children from Stepney Causeway and other vulnerable areas were transferred to the country and instructed how to use gas masks. Children witnessed aircraft shot down in dogfights and some had their homes blown up by enemy bombs.

In October 1939, two sets of twin boys were taken into care by Barnardo's when their father was lost in the sinking of the *HMS Courageous.* The summer camp for Russell Cotes Nautical School at Poole, Dorset, which consisted of large white tents was decimated by a stick of nine bombs the night after the boys had left.

A party of boys were due to leave for Australia in November but this was cancelled. After the *Strathaird* arrived in March 1939, with 35 boys and 18 girls, farewelled in London by the Duke of Devonshire and welcomed by His Excellency the Governor in Sydney, there would be no further child migrant parties until November 1947.

An evacuation party, London 1937

Australians and other member countries of the Commonwealth offered homes to orphans and refugees and sent donations. Mercantile Mutual Staff Patriotic and Benefit Fund was one of these donors.   At this time, ten shillings would feed a child for a fortnight.

'Australia will mind the baby while the Allies battle for life', read one headline. In the ABC Weekly Ernestine Hill wrote,

'This country more than another is a paradise for the child - yet many a time in its great loneliness, I have travelled a thousand miles without seeing one! The young are easily adaptable - they know no dividing line or nation or class or caste. They learn a language in a few short months where the older people stammer through and cling to worn traditions... Excellent and inspiring work has been done in the past by child migration societies in this country. Such schemes as Dr Barnardo's Homes and the Fairbridge Farm Schools speak for themselves in ideals and achievements. Unfortunately they are as yet in their infancy in comparison with what they yet will be. In the past 20 years the Barnardo Homes have brought to Australia 2000 children - to Canada 30 000 - and the Fairbridge Farms 1000. These have all been carefully selected little Britishers, boys and girls 100 per cent in health and mentality. They have been a magnificent success. Two or three of our child migrants have already won Rhodes Scholarships. Many are now in khaki fighting for the Empire in need...What finer migration policy has the New World ever known? What more magnificent record to write for the future than a national work unique in history, if we can extend this loving kindness to those children of Europe in need, whose fathers - and mothers - died in the cause of our freedom. Australia, land of youth, calls to the sorrowing youth of the world'.

123

Unlike migrants of the 20's, 30's and 40's who went straight onto the land or into domestic science, children whose attainments merited it proceeded to a High School or Agricultural College. Barnardo's now had a number of successful young people to its credit. A Barnardo boy was elected School Captain, another came first in his year (of 150 pupils), and two more lads from Picton qualified for entry. These lads would eventually become teachers of agricultural subjects and enter the Public Service.

Amongst the old girls' successes was one who was appointed Matron of a hospital in the Islands, and another who was on the staff of a leading City Business College.

One old boy wrote saying that he owned his own farm on the North Coast. Another wrote:
'I send my sincere thanks and best wishes to the Homes for the advancement of its purpose and for the way it has treated me. Where would I have been today if it were not for the Homes?'

Yet another wrote: 'I am enclosing £1 as a donation I am still in the same job (12 years) have saved £300 (in addition to nearly £200 in my trust account at the Sydney Office), and have a small car of my own'.

Amongst a number of similar letters from employers, are the following:
'X is the very best man I have, and I hope to make him overseer when he is 21. He is still keen to get married, and when he is able I will provide him with a home.'

'Y, an old Barnardo boy, is still with us, and has been for sixteen years'.

'I would very much like to take this opportunity of conveying to you the esteem in which Z was held amongst the townspeople. Of gentlemanly demeanour, clean habits, open and straight forward manner and of a most lovable nature, he is missed by all. If Z is the average type of boy your Association is concerned with, then you are indeed to be congratulated'.

124

The Forties
The War Years

Those who served

126

Two of the younger lads who were out in their first jobs, greet two of the old boys serving with the 2nd AIF. They are at the annual Christmas party at Barnardo House, Burwood on December 14th. In uniform, l to r: Pte George Burford and Gunner Herbert Sunley. Younger boys, l to r: Allan Moore and Stanley Baldwin.

The name of a Barnardo boy appeared on the first published list of those who gave their lives for others. In NSW earlier Barnardo migrants were now old enough to serve. More and more orphans appeared as the war gathered pace. The NSW branch of the Association was dependent on the London based organisation for an annual amount of £14 000.

Barnardo's didn't escape the Blitz and the rain of bombs which fell on East London. In the autumn of 1940 Nazi fire bombs fell on Nos 2-26 and the whole of the top floor was gutted. Large reserves of clothing and toys put by for Christmas were lost - the publications department was destroyed, and the general office suffered considerable damage by water.

Ten days later a high explosive bomb struck the food stores and wrecked the Resident Superintendent's house. With the coming of war in 1939 the Receiving Houses the Ever-Open-Door, and the Marie Hilton Creche closed and the children were evacuated. The closure was for the duration of the war - but they were never to open again. In 1940, No 4 The Causeway opened as a working lads hostel and remained as such until 1966.

Of about 2 000 child migrants who had come to Australia, 1 079 were over twenty-one years and mostly still in touch with the Homes. Chairman of the Committee was still Sir Arthur Rickard and Chairman of the Executive Committee Dr E W Fairfax. The Superintendent of the Farm School was Captain R D Rees RNR (retired) helped by Mrs Rees. The Matron of the Girl's Hostel and Training Home was Miss N Dobbie. That year, the boys went to Wollongong for a holiday while the girls went to Dee Why.

127

Lord Gowrie, the Patron, and Lady Gowrie visited the Farm School, where 360 additional acres of land had been acquired to run sheep. Lady Gowrie said, 'In all the madness and fury of a distracted world, it is good to turn to those practical examples of practical Christianity which still remain to give proof of the essential goodness of human nature'.

The Children

Children are always touched by war. In 1940, 125 000 children were admitted. Two hundred refugee Czechoslovakian children were admitted to Barnardo's in the UK, in 1939.

In Sydney, Lady Gowrie said at a charity performance of *The Boy from Barnardo's* at the Civic and Capitol Theatres,'...the admission of children to Homes in the UK has increased from five a day in peacetime to double that figure as a direct result of the war'.

The Mothers of the Children from the Forties

For all the long-lasting tragedy that the war brought, there were benefits. Women's existence was revolutionalised throughout the western world and in Russia. Their role as mothers was significantly altered.

Women were empowered by the war. Faced with the need for manpower to be replaced and support for the armed forces, governments reluctantly turned to womanpower. In Australia, concerns voiced by Mr Forde, Minister for the Army and Mr Drakeford, Minister for the Air, about womanpower were proved groundless. After a cautious beginning, service chiefs were asking for more and more. By mid-1945 a total of 66 000 women was serving. The Services tested women who previously had no yardstick with which to measure their potential. When it was time to pick up their lives again, women had a new strength of purpose, and sense of their worth.

Women, realising their intelligence and worth, translated them into money. Having their own money meant independence of action. Life had changed for ever for mothers-to-be.

Copus, Anne, 'I came out in 1939 aged 13 and my old grandmother came down to Tilbury to see me off. The vastness of the journey was awesome, I was seasick all the way and all I could think was, 'How ever will I find my way back?' My dad had been in WW1 and had a plate in his head. I couldn't write to anyone because I didn't have any addresses and I felt a yearning always, I was lost and lonely. Eventually, after about twelve years, I found my sister, who had had a little boy.

After Burwood,I was working in Canberra as a housekeeper and missed the girl's company, so I joined the AWAS as NF46594 . I was in Ordnance, handing out petrol allowances.

From a letter in The Australian Women's Digest, July 1947: 'The Land Army, Mr Robertson told me, did a wonderful job. No doubt about it, they were a grand lot of girls— tigers for toil and always cheerful. Don't know what the farmers would have done without them. Well, Girls, I suppose we should be grateful for these kind words. But I couldn't help thinking...a kiss on the hand may make you feel very good but a diamond bracelet lasts for ever. Growing vegetables for Army contracts, Mr Robertson employed two men and four Land Girls; his wage bill was about 30% less for identical work than it would have been if his six employees had all been male. He's a nice man and a good boss and I like him. But one can't avoid the reflection that it was a pretty good war for him, at your expense'.

Although post-war women had to relinquish their jobs to nurse physically and mentally damaged husbands, fathers and brothers, they never lost their newfound awareness. If they could not sustain a career at that time, they returned to the workforce seven years later when their children were at school. They urged their daughters to become high-achievers, not merely dependent on the sometimes mythical 'breadwinner'. This meant that although illegitimacy was still a stigma, there was the beginnings of a change in attitude towards unsupported mothers.

Families had been fragmented and housing was at a premium, so support networks had been disrupted, but a woman could rent a flat or house alone without being viewed as a 'scarlet woman'.

Young women entering marriage and motherhood had a new status compared with previous decades. Uncertainty of income, shortage of housing, the high cost of living and improved education meant the average couple would have 2.4 children, easier on the woman's health and allowing for some self determination. Long engagements were still the norm with eyebrows raised at anything less than seven months, and illegitimacy still a stigma, but 21 per cent of couples had a child before the marriage was 8 months old, which would have previously been thought shocking.

Post-war Australia was desperate for good young people to rebuild their nation. Migrants from the UK were keenly sought and would now be encouraged to reach their potential rather than used as slave labour.

Children are our Future

The UK and Australian governments of decimated populations reached the same conclusion - they had lost swathes of young people and their children were the future. The UK government policy changed diametrically from exporting children as migrants from crowded and socially inadequate conditions, to prizing, supporting and protecting them. In 1944 it was stipulated that orphans who lost both parents in the war must remain in Britain 'until they are of an age to make a choice for themselves'. Pensions Minister Sir Walter Womersley was made a guardian of all children by parliament.

In 1945, Malcolm Delevigne, Chairman of the Council of Dr Barnardo's London, stated, '...the standard demanded by Australia (for child migrants) was 'physically fit with an IQ of 90 and

Norman Fullerton leads Tinker while Mr Heath guides the plough

freedom from hereditary taint'...the result of this stipulation has been that we have chosen the cream of our children and by sending them to Australia to be trained for primary industry we have in fact deprived children of more than average intelligence of the possibility of obtaining higher education and getting higher skilled situations in the UK.

Assurances were sought from the Commonwealth and New South Wales governments that 'if children of a high standard of intelligence and physical fitness are sent out, the children will be given the opportunity of obtaining a higher education and if they wish of entering industrial or professional walks of life'.

132

'..the serious decline in the Australian birthrate has created a problem of the gravest nature', (Acting Prime Minister Mr Forde in the Sydney Morning Herald in June 1944).

The *Melbourne Herald*, declared 'History will some day reveal how close Australia came to being overrun. We may not be given another chance'.

Dr Fairfax, January 10th 1946, to Prime Minister Chifley... 'I enclose a map... ...from the map you will learn how and where to place emigres in climatic and economic conditions approximating to those places which they have come from. (The map, covered in red dots shows almost all areas of the UK)'.

In August 19th 1946 State and Commonwealth Ministers considered all aspects of migration. A following Premier's Conference made the decision to raise the age limit for boys and girls aged 17-19 to be brought from England.

Dr E W Fairfax Chairman, Executive Committee NSW Branch Dr Barnardo's Homes wrote to Minister Calwell in 1946, 'It has been our experience that the most appropriate age for the children to arrive in Australia is between seven and ten years. They are then more adaptable to their new surroundings for education and training in agriculture and domestic work'.

The phrase relating to children's 'training in agricultural and domestic work' does not relate well to Barnardo's new policies, which had been in place since the 1940's. Girls at Burwood, for instance, were trained according to their abilities and ambitions and given vocational guidance tests. The Barnardo's authorities were keenly conscious of the need for care for the sixteen to twenty-one year olds in the unsettled war years, but they encouraged the girls to treat Burwood like their home and bring visitors. Barnardo House Burwood accommodated school girls, trainees and girls in employment as well as young women in the Services. Girls proceeded to Teacher's College and into the world of commerce, under the direction of the Manpower Department, they no longer automatically entered domestic work as in the 20's and 30's.

The Commonwealth Government, anxious about the falling birthrate, announced a plan to bring out 17 000 child migrants a year for three years but details of the plan were not made public. The UK did not respond to the proposal. The Allies were fighting for survival and surrounded by death, held on to their children. No child migrant parties would arrive until 1947.

133

Those who Served

From *Night and Day, The Wide Horizon, Barnardo News* from *Near and Far:*

The following letter recently reached us from a Chaplain serving with the Australian Forces, after his liberation from a Japanese prison camp:

Several times in my life I have come across boys from your fine Institution, first when I used to visit the Dr Barnardo's Home farm at Picton, NSW man years ago: secondly when I trained at College for the Church of England ministry with a former boy from one of the English Homes, The Reverend Leslie Crossman now of NSW and then again when in Thailand in the thick of the Siamese jungle. So this letter is a tribute to the lads you train and in honour of one of them whom I laid to rest.
We both were prisoners of war building the infamous Thai Burma railway for the Japanese and it was at Toncham South jungle camp in Siam that cholera struck the area. I do not know from what Home Sapper Rehbein came but I felt I should write to you so that perhaps the younger lads might be inspired by the courage and endurance of Barnardo boys under difficulties and danger.

134

Dr Raymond Green, Vice Chairman of the Executive Committee of the NSW Branch of Dr Barnardo's Homes says farewell to the boys: l to r: Reg Cole Herbert Sunley John Westoff Henry Wheeler John Parkinson Albert Gabriel

135

By 1943 more than 4 000 old Barnardo's boys were serving in the Empire Forces and Mercantile Marine. There were 200 boys from NSW Homes in the AIF, 30 in the RAAF and 12 in the RAN and Mercantile Marine. The auxiliary services ammunition factories were employing 16 Barnardo girls. Sir Arthur Rickard, stated that children already brought to Australia had proved that they were an asset to the country.

Charles Jenkins

Charles Jenkins, orphaned when he was six years old, arrived in 1939 in the *Strathaird* aged 13. His younger sister Lilian wrote to him regularly and when he was 21, Charles sent her £12 to enable her to emigrate. Charles convinced Mr Ladd at Mowbray Park Farm that he was not suitable for farming, and went to work first at Newcastle, then Annandale. In 1943 he joined the RAAF as a fitter, ACI 136586 and served at Townsville until he was discharged in 1946 as LAC Jenkins.

The late Charles Jenkins LAC 136586. He was orphaned and put into Dr Barnardo's Homes when his grandfather became too old to care for him.

Meeting up again on Founder's Day while in the AIF:
Ted Howard Ossie Davies Bill Copus Bill Alexander Joe Andrews

141

The Blitz

Barnardo Headquarters was bombed several times. High explosive bombs damaged the Mercantile Marine Training School and the Southsea (Portsmouth) Branch. The Northampton Branch was damaged and the Birmingham 'Ever Open Door' hit by incendiary and delayed action bombs which, fortunately did a minimum of damage on account of prompt action in dealing with them. A large number of incendiary bombs were dropped on the Girls Village Home. The hospital and new massage hut were badly damaged and two cottages set on fire. Clapton was rendered uninhabitable by a high explosive bomb. Other branches suffered to varying degrees but the children were all evacuated and not one life was lost in the raids.

"Strike Hard"

Bob Cooper

Bob Cooper and John Savage in Beirut Lebanon August 1941 after the severe fighting and subsequent fighting of the Vichy French

The Three Musketeers

Captain PS Curry MC OAM, Officer Commanding Platoon Commander over the Kokoda Trail:

Our three 2/33 Battalion Barnardo members - John Savage, Bob Cooper and Charlie Wilson were popular members of the Unit although I did not know Charlie personally. Both John and Bob attained the rank of Sergeant. Bob was in my platoon during the Owen Stanley Campaign and to me he, like John, was a great soldier. The tributes to Bob when he died in August, 1992, speak volumes. He was twice Mentioned in Dispatches (MID).John was one of the select handful of members of the Battalion who served in all four of the campaigns in which the Unit was involved, Syria, Kokoda Trail, Lae, Ramu Valley and Balikpapan in Borneo, <u>without losing a day in action.</u> Both were fine soldiers and a credit to their adopted country.

From the editor of *Mud and Blood,* Captain ML Roberts: Bob joined the Battalion at Kilo 89 in Palestine and was posted to 11 Platoon B Coy. At that time I was the Platoon Commander and remained so throughout the Syrian campaign. Bob was a tower of strength throughout this action and remained with 11 Platoon during the war in the Pacific. He was mentioned in despatches in the Kokoda show and was wounded at Gona on 29 November, 1942. He served in the Lae, Ramu Valley and then in Borneo where he was again mentioned in despatches, finishlng the war as Sgt. Cooper, well respected, a man amongst men.

Major Dug Cullen MC: Bobby Cooper, was one of our most distinguished soldiers, twice being mentloned in despatches and once wounded. There was more than one occasion when a higher award should have been his but he was always to be denied a decoration. His valour and leadershlp during the Opus-Operator battle in Borneo is a good example of how high command can wrongly assess unit citations. Bobby's courage and quick thinking are legend among those who served with him. He led from the front with great determination and without thought of his own safety. The warmth of his personality, his sense of humour, his encouragement to reinforcements, his aversion to humbug all gave confidence to those who followed him.

The treatment was good at Barnardos, punishment was fair, if you got the strap you didn't moan about it, took it like a man.

Ernie Rowe

July 1937 on board the Otranto, leaving Tilbury. Ernie is far left at the back, feeling very excited.

148

I was born in Endersley Street, St Pancras in the maternity wing of the Royal Free Hospital, a true Cockney. I lost my mother when I was eight. Father had terrible wounds from WW1 and lost his job because of them. I went to Stepney Causeway and then to the Brighton and Hove Orphan Boys Home and then to Barkingside. When I was about 14 they asked if we wanted to go to Canada, Rhodesia or Australia. We kids decided that Canada was the one to ask for because if you didn't like it you could stow away and get home easily but if you went to Sydney you'd never get away - they'd find you at Melbourne.

I thought I was going to Canada and thought it strange we left from Tilbury because ships bound for the New World left from Liverpool. We asked Mr Stables at Australia House before we left and Mr Bertram who was in charge of our party where we were going but they were coy about answering. When we went ashore at Gibraltar and sailed down the Suez Canal we worked it out for ourselves! I went straight to Scheyville Agricultural School near Windsor in New South Wales and then aged about 14, onto the land - keep and ten shillings.

I worked for a while in Pitt Town for people from Gallway and it was awful, hoeing manually all day, living in a hut with two other boys, never allowed in the house. The place was lousy with snakes. I was bitten by a red bellied black near the hut. 'There are more people die of shock than snake bite', said an old-timer. I got the sack for not working hard enough, but they were never satisfied.

The *Otranto* group were good mates right through four months training at Scheyville but we lost touch afterwards. I was the first to go. Although my first job didn't work out, my second job working for a poultry farmer in Canberra delivering eggs in a Model T Ford was fine. We had two huts for four boys outside. It was good tucker.

I worked in Canberra for an English poultry farmer for sixteen months, a very good boss. When war broke out I volunteered straight away. My boss, Tom Horn, said there was always a place for me there. As I was in primary industry, I did not have to go in the army and could have stayed on the land. He was very proud that I was the first person in Canberra to volunteer. I joined the 2/33 Battalion, staying with them until peace. I have mixed feelings about the war. I was personally responsible for the deaths of seventeen people by mortar fire in the Syrian campaign. I don't feel good about it.

Gaza guard
Christmas 1940

Outside Tripoli,
Syria 1941

Bayonet practice Beirut
Jirga near Gaza 1940

I always kept in touch with my dad through letters, except once during the war years when the Red Cross were looking for me in Tripoli on his behalf. He hadn't heard from me for over six months. I was curious about my family and eventually traced my people through the Salvation Army, who have very good records worldwide. I found three cousins and visited them. Rowe is a Cornish name and there are a lot in Cornwall.

Home to me is 3 Avenue Road, Tottenham where my sons were born.

149

Barnardo's were like my mother and father to me in my early years.

Gerald Griggs

I was fostered out one week after birth in 1923 in Norfolk and stayed there happily until I was nine years old. I went to Stepney Causeway and then to different homes, until I was eleven, when I sailed for Australia in the *Barrabool*. I arrived in 1934 and went to Mowbray Park and then onto a dairy farm, where I was treated like one of the family. Barnardo's asked for my wages to be raised from ten shillings to twelve shillings and sixpence, but my employers could not do this as the depression was in full swing, so I left for a wheat and sheep station. I was unhappy there and jumped a train to Sydney where I joined the Army at Moore Park Depot.

I was up at Berrimah near Darwin, prior to Japan entering the war where the camp had to be built from scratch, and there in 1941 during the first raid, firing at the Japanese bombers.

After discharge, I was sent to Heidelberg Hospital with malaria. I later worked as a cook, kitchen hand, bus driver porter and railway guard.

I met Gwen and we stayed married happily until I was unfortunately widowed. We had six children. Of these, five remain, with 13 grandchildren and two great grandchildren.

Anne Copus

*Anne Copus with
three AWAS friends*

I came out in 1939 aged 13. My dad had been in WW1 and had a plate in his head. When we lost our mother, my grandmother, who was 70, was our only relative. She put us in because she just found it too much looking after the three of us. She used to visit us at Barkingside and was always made welcome by the authorities. My sister and I were sent to Middlesborough. They used to stand us in a line for castor oil. I had a flair for dancing and looked like Shirley Temple. I was allowed to go on outings with benefactors. They wanted to adopt me and I don't know what happened but they didn't. My brother was adopted out from Barkingside and I didn't meet up with him until he was 60. Grandmother came down to Tilbury to see me off in the *Strathaird*. The vastness of the journey was awesome. I was seasick all the way and all I could think was, 'How ever will I find my way back?' I couldn't write to anyone because I didn't have any addresses and I felt a yearning always, was lost and lonely. Eventually, after about twelve years, found my sister, who had had a little boy. After being trained at Burwood, I was working in Canberra as a housekeeper and missed the girl's company, so I joined the AWAS as NF46594 . I was in Ordnance, handing out petrol allowances.

Arthur Hook

From an un-named newspaper article:
Eight 'Kids' Joined Up, So Mother Got Busy

Mrs Hook and her family are going all out to defeat the Nazis. While mother stands all day at her work at a Birmingham aircraft factory, eight of her twelve children are in the Services or the Land Army.

Mrs Hook is 54 years old now. When her husband died eight years ago, her eldest son Eric Thomas was only 19. The youngest 'kids' were still toddling around the kitchen.

Deprived of her mate and bread-winner, Mrs. Hook has had a constant struggle to make ends meet. Somehow she managed to rear her children into healthy young men and women.

THEY LOOK REAL SMART
Now Erlc Thomas, (27) is a quartermaster sergeant in the Royal Army Ordnance Corps. Rose (25) is in the ATS; Arnold (24) is an Army corporal serving in Africa. and Norman (22) is doing splendid work with the Paratroops in Tunisia.

Jean (21), Christina (19), and Amy (17) are in the Land Army, and 'they look real smart in their green jerseys; and brown breeches,' their proud mother told me. John (16) is a sailor.

Two of the younger boys are in Australia another girl is being brought up by an aunt and the other girl, a Girl Guide, is the only member of the family who lives at home.   As one child after another joined the Services, Mrs Hook grew very lonely. But it was no use crying.

'Why cry? Why not do my bit too?' said this courageous woman.

So she offered her services to the factory where her husband had worked. She has been there eighteen months now and spent sixteen of them on night work. Now she works from 6.30 am to 7.30 at night and wouldn't miss it for worlds.

Her daughter in law is employed at the same factory. A simple story this - but it contains a glowing lesson for many.

Mrs Hook's life, sacrificed to the job of bringing up a family - of which she is justly proud - is now given without stint to toil in the war industry.

Tony Edwards 23400, Ken Church's foster brother: I came out aged 11 in the *Ballarat*. I joined the Navy as a stoker and served on both oil fired and coal fired ships.

Tony Edwards

In June, 1938, I left Fairbridge for my first job on a property out from Katanning, in the wheat belt of WA. I landed on my feet for my boss, Mr Stan Holding, and his wife, Alice, treated me like family. In March 1939, my boss left the land. It was depression time and wheat was down to one shilling and fourpence a bushel and wool at tenpence a pound. (Boycott Japan was in progress at that time).

I returned to Fairbridge where I worked for my keep alone, the going rate twenty one shillings a week. I lived at the Old Fairbridgian Club House except for six weeks I spent on a dairy farm, out from Harvey, keeping the job open for a kid, Bill Brooks, who had gone to hospital.

In June, 1939, I got my call up for the Navy. No more cows but a new and interesting life, something I knew I could make into a career. On the 4th July, 1939, I was sworn in at HMAS *Leeuwin*, the local naval depot in Fremantle.

I received the King's shilling, a custom still observed in 1939, plus ten shillings expenses and a rail warrant to Flinders Naval Depot at Westernport, Victoria. It may sound trite but it was the proudest day of my life until I married in December, 1942.

I missed being drafted to HMAS *Sydney* with all my mates and instead, in January, 1940, I found myself part of a draft of Australian ratings taking passage aboard the battleship, *HMS Ramillies*, to join *HMAS Hobart* stationed

HMAS Hobart

HMS Ramillies

HMAS Sydney

in the East Indies. The *HMS Ramillies* was part (a big part with 8 x 15" guns) of the escort taking the first ANZAC convoy to WWII.

In January, 1941, *HMAS Hobart* was serving in Australian waters prior to going to the Mediterranean; in June 1941, and there outside Wynyard Station in George St, Sydney by prior arrangement, I met this huge fella in a Tanky's battledress part of the Australian Armoured Division. Ken Church and I were finally reunited.

2 September 1945, JAPAN SURRENDERS

General MacArthur stated: My earnest hope—indeed the hope of all mankind—that from this solemn occasion a better world shall emerge out of the blood and carnage of the past, a world founded upon faith and understanding, a world dedicated to the dignity of man and the fulfilment of his most cherished wish for freedom, tolerance and justice.

154

INSTRUMENT OF SURRENDER

Signed at TOKYO BAY, JAPAN at ____
on the ____ SECOND ____ day of ____ S____

重光葵

By Command and in behalf of ____
and the Japanese Government.

We, acting by command of and in behalf of the Emperor of Japan, the Japanese Government and the Japanese Imperial General Headquarters, hereby accept the provisions set forth in the declaration issued by the heads of the Governments of the United States, China and Great Britain on 26 July 1945, at Potsdam, and subsequently adhered to by the Union of Soviet Socialist Republics, which four powers are hereafter referred to as the Allied Powers.

梅津美治郎

By Command and in behalf of ____
Imperial General Headquarters

We hereby proclaim the unconditional surrender to the Allied Powers of the Japanese Imperial General Headquarters and of all Japanese armed forces and all armed forces under Japanese control wherever situated

We hereby command all Japanese forces wherever situated and the Japanese people to cease hostilities forthwith, to preserve and save from damage all ships, aircraft, and military and civil property and to comply with all requirements which may be imposed by the Supreme Commander for the Allied Powers or by agencies of the Japanese Government at his direction.

Accepted at TOKYO BAY, JAPAN at ____
on the ____ SECOND ____ day of ____ SE____
for the United States, Republic of China, United K____
Union of Soviet Socialist Republics, and in the inter____
United Nations at war with Japan.

Douglas MacArthur
Supreme Commander for the Al____

We hereby command the Japanese Imperial General Headquarters to issue at once orders to the Commanders of all Japanese forces and all forces under Japanese control wherever situated to surrender unconditionally themselves and all forces under their control.

C.W. Nimitz
United States Representative

We hereby command all civil, military and naval officials to obey and enforce all proclamations, orders and directives deemed by the Supreme Commander for the Allied Powers to be proper to effectuate this surrender and issued by him or under his authority and we direct all such officials to remain at their posts and to continue to perform their non-combatant duties unless specifically

徐永昌
Republic of China Representative

Bruce Fraser
United Kingdom Representative

After 1 364 days, 5 hours and 14 minutes, World War ll, Pacific, ended officially at 0904 September 2, 1945, with the signing of the *Instrument of Surrender* on the battleship USS *Missouri* anchored in Tokyo Bay. It was the costliest war in history.

Sid Bines

George S Bines, known as Sid, arrived in the *Balranald* on 19th August 1926.

SG Bines 14723 RAAF, is one of the participants in the photograph below of one of the Japanese surrender points. Sid was a whizz with radios, self-taught, and in great demand by the English pilots leaving their base for sorties over Germany.
Sid became a successful farmer in Australia, growing grapes at Glenorie and a substantial donor to Barnardo's. As he became older, he had difficulty walking and Bill Moverley used to visit him with a flagon of sherry about once a fortnight. The dog would bark and Sid would sing out, 'Have you got my sherry?'

155

Roland
Paxton

Roly, Farm Manager, at City Tatts in 1986

156

Roland Paxton still farms on a property at Raleigh near Coffs Harbour.   He came to Australia from a village in Hertfordshire England as a 17 year-old. to escape the unpalatable prospect of having to commute to crowded London to work. He attended Hawkesbury Agricultural College and worked on cattle properties.

Roly was an Air Force navigator in WW11, and lost an eardrum. He worked with Dr Barnardo's children at Mowbray Park Farm Picton from 1942 to 1952 and finally bought his dairy farm, which had always been a dream of his and Kit's.   Roly was a great farmer and an almost universal favourite with the trainees. At his interview, Wilfred Fairfax and a few others asked, 'Could you teach boys things?' 'Yes', he answered. They asked Roly's first wife, Kit, 'Have you any experience in child welfare?' 'I was one of thirteen', she said. Kit, much loved by the children, contracted hydatis on the liver in 1952, losing most of her liver. Kit died at Raleigh after a long fight against cancer in 1969, 17 years after leaving Picton.

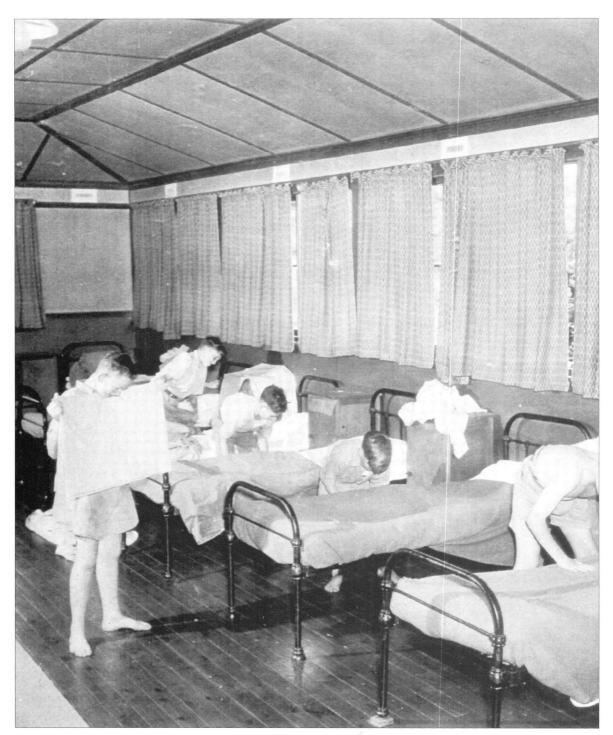

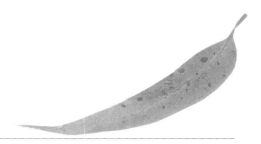

THE DEPRESSION
Roly wrote the following concerning the Big Brother movement, which like the Barnardo migration policy gave young men a chance to emigrate and work on the land, with a 'Big Brother', between the end of the Great Depression and the beginning of the early threats of war from Hitler:
In my estimation the Big Brother movement is almost an ideal institution. The young settler feels less lonely, is rather 'bucked' by the fact that his personal welfare is the consideration of an individual and not the vague protection of a Board or Department.   Also this fact helps in procuring the right type of boy from England— the son of parents who want their son to do well and are probably anxious lest he be stranded. A word as to the right type of boy. An English lad, starting farming at the age of 16 out here, is starting with a big handicap. Success is due to a large extent on the opposition met with. The Australian boy is almost as good a farmer at 16 as his father, and this is the opposition the raw 'new chum' has to face. I think the greatest drawback to the newcomer is his lack of observation. All cattle look the same, so do horses, grasses, paddocks and trees. Personally when I look back on all the stupid mistakes and the extra labour that fell to my lot in the first two years I wonder how I muddled through whole! The best type of boy is the chap who is physically fit likes work and plenty of it, and, just as important, has a SECONDARY EDUCATION. This fact alone has helped me tremendously. It restored my rather battered self respect and gave me an advantage over most of the opposition.

What I lacked in experience and observation I made up with my better education. When the depression was first felt, I polished my trigonometry and did amateur surveying for irrigation, ditches, grades for private roads and measuring blocks of land for contract hand-clearing, &c. A smattering of chemistry and electricity helped me a lot. Veterinary surgeons are scarce in the bush and their fees are not commensurate with the value of stock. So I 'swatted' animal husbandry with the help of the 'Tech.' I now have a handy but quite illegal, veterinary practice, on 'no cure—no pay' basis. A smattering of bookkeeping kept my station hand job when most of the other local men were put off Now, after 11 years in the bush, I am (or think I am) as good as any local man at the job,-plus extra knowledge on a good many extra subjects. So the boy with the Secondary Education is more likely to succeed when the going gets rough. To make the Big Brother Movement ideal, I would add three months of training for the boy on arrival in Australia. This gives them time to assimilate Australian ideology and to feel and look less conspicuously 'Pommies'.

159

PERSONAL EXPERIENCE OF EMPLOYERS
They work hard themselves and expect you to do the same and though sometimes I have felt as if I have been exploited, I have credited it to experience gained. The best employer is the owner farmer rather than the share or tenant-farmer. The reason is obvious. The owner farmer is combining making a living with improving his property. He is engaged in, say, dairying and in between times in fencing, scrub felling, ringbarking etc. The tenant farmer or share farmer is concentrating on getting as much out of the property as possible.

PROSPECTS OF THE LITTLE BROTHERS
This a possible fly in the ointment. There is a big demand for boys on farms, especially now - the wages are from 15s to 25s. When the lad is 20-22 he rightly thinks that he is entitled to a bigger wage. But the farmer can't afford it. It is probably the biggest problem that the Little Brother has to face. The following are open to him: (1) fencing, felling, brushing etc. (2) Share-farming. (3) Tenant-farming. (4) Selecting. I will rule out the possibility of the boy buying a place because if he has saved £50 up to this period he has done pretty well.
CONTRACT WORK
This shows better returns-generally from £3 to £4 per week- but the amount of lost time between jobs and shifting of camps is enormous and the average weekly income would be little better than 25 shillings per week.
SHARE FARMING
Undoubtedly the best way out of the trouble-it affords the opportunity of trying oneself out and you stand to lose nothing but your labour. But there is not nearly enough share farming to go round. So much so that dairy farms, usually shared out on a 50-50 basis are now tendered for-some share-farmers offering the owner 14 shillings in the pound.

TENANT FARMING
These are usually let by tender-and usually someone tenders more than a reasonable amount and has to work hard for a pittance. But, apart from this, a considerable amount of capital is needed, about £400 for an average plant.
The one answer to the gap between farm hand and farm owner is CLOSER SETTLEMENT. In this district there are vast areas of undeveloped scrub land held by men who won't develop it. The Forestry holds a lot more and more still is being used to only a fraction of its productiveness as grazing country for cattle. In conclusion may every Little Brother have as good Big Brother as I have - who is still carrying on although officially his job finished eight years ago.

It would take a good middle-class family to treat the boys better than we did at Mowbray Park. My three kids were treated exactly the same as the boys, - same pocket money, everything. They say now that they were the happiest days of their lives. I worked with Captain Rees who had been Captain of the *Hood*.

There were 12 to 15 boys in a cottage with a cottage mother who cooked and looked after them. A psychologist helped boys with emotional problems after leaving Britain. I remember one sad incident. Little Willie Vincent used to get up early and kill rabbits. He got two shillings a skin. One day he complained of stomach ache and we feared appendicitis so we took him into Camden Hospital. On that day there was a terrible motorcar accident on Razorback Mountain and the hospital was swamped with cases. Little Willie couldn't be treated straight away and his appendix burst. Unfortunately penicillin was only available for the troops and he died.

I used to give Farm Lectures after tea at night during which the poultry would be locked up and the horses put in the stables. Usually the boys did not volunteer for this. One night, all their hands shot up with requests 'to lock up'. I realised the girls were parading to and fro in the lit windows of their cottages on the hill.

Resumption
of migration

While travel restrictions kept the sons of millionaires at home, the child migrants went out for a bright future

Sir Arthur Rickard wrote in the foreword to the *NSW Annual Report* for the year ending December 1945, ' we enter upon a period when it is hoped that we may peacefully further and develop in Australia the great work of the Barnardo organisation. The imperative need for increased population has been forced into the position of priority as a national problem, and it is generally recognised that juveniles of both sexes are the most desirable immigrants'.

The 1947 arrivals

In August 1947, Barnardos in London made arrangements for 40 children aged eight to 15 from Dr Barnardo's Homes to go to Australia on the *Ormonde* escorted by Mr and Mrs Nash, Mr Allen, Miss Talbot-Rice, Miss Windibank and Miss Williams. Twenty would go to Picton and twenty to domestic science studies at Burwood, attending Croydon or Burwood public schools.

The girls arrived on 17th November and were greeted by Matron Dobbie and the Mayor of Burwood, who spoke of the vocational guidance tests the girls would take. They would be given the opportunity to matriculate and go on to university.

From the Press: Little Peter Wetherill, sunshine of the party has a wide, happy beam for everybody

Peter Walton
1947

Aged 11, Peter wanted to be a boundary rider

Swimming and making rafts below the dam,

My mother Alice left her husband, Ralph Walton in 1934 and went to live with George Weatherill, a widower who owned a chemist shop. George died in 1939. Three children were born to Alice and George: Peter, George and Patricia. By December 1941 the children were put in Barnardo's care due to the ill-health of our mother.

Nothing was ever explained to me. It was not until 1998 when I received my admission papers that I learned my mother left her first husband, Ralph because of ill-treatment. I believe I have three older brothers who live in Grimsby. She fell in love with George Weatherill, my father, but changed my surname after his death to comply with the

authorities. I was falsely registered as the son of Ralph Walton. This made it very difficult in tracing my relatives. I didn't manage to meet my brother George in his lifetime, but I did meet Patricia.

After the three of us, aged five, six and seven, were put into Barnardo's, we were fostered to three different families in the same village, Wetherden, Suffolk. We went to the same school but otherwise did not see each other. The other two were happy and stayed but I was in a bad situation for two years. Inspectors wrote of it as 'unsatisfactory', with the foster children being beaten, an anonymous letter to the police confirming this suspicion, the NSPCC

Pauline, Pat, Peter, Susan and Tracey, reunited in 1999

complaining and my foster father being described as a 'surly looking' man. They tried to change my name to 'Michael' and my report reads of my being 'cowed'. Another report mentions my foster mother 'takes her pleasures sadly' since her house was bombed, she seems very harsh and could not understand a boy'. She 'makes her boys difficult. Their whole nature seems to change after being a while with her'. In June 1945 all the children were moved and the home closed. They told me I had no relatives, that they had all died. Six months after coming to Australia I was told I did have brothers and sisters.

At Kingston, they asked if we wanted to go to Canada or Australia. I said 'Australia, because it starts with 'A'. 12 months later, we sailed and I really enjoyed the trip and loved being at Picton. I worked on dairy farms and joined the army in 1956.

I have a happy marriage but some of the difficulties were caused by my being conscious of over-discipline with my two great children, (who are still with us). I had two years of cruelty with the foster parents and no model family life to help me and my career in the Army took me away for long periods of time. I came out of the army in 1977 and worked in stores and warehousing, finding it difficult to settle at one thing for very long. I retired in 1998. My eldest boy is a courier, the youngest an accountant. We have two lovely grand-daughters. All the harsh times I had as a child, the most harrowing times were those I spent in Vietnam as a S/sgt.

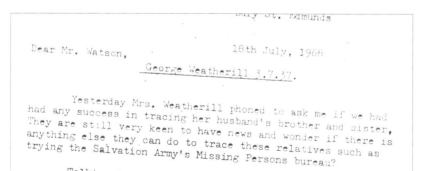

Bury St. Edmunds

Dear Mr. Watson,   18th July, 1968

George Weatherill 3.7.37.

Yesterday Mrs. Weatherill phoned to ask me if we had had any success in tracing her husband's brother and sister. They are still very keen to have news and wonder if there is anything else they can do to trace these relatives such as trying the Salvation Army's Missing Persons bureau?

Talking to Mrs. Weatherill I learnt that George is very confused about his history. Somebody told him his father lived in Grimsby and was killed in the war when George was about 3 years of age - but someone else told him his father deserted his mother and is still alive. I feel we should tell George what we know about his background and how he came into our care so will you please send me a copy of his history ? I hope Mr. Price in Australia is eventually able to contact the brother Peter.

Beryl Wright
1947

Beryl is the laughing figure in the foreground

My mother died of cancer, leaving my brother and father who were working for Manpower and could not care for me and my sister and an older sister who had just married aged 22. She and her new husband gave me and my sister £1 in silver threepenny bits each. I was ten years old. I went down to Ilford and bought a tiny violin. My sister and I were put into Barnardos. When I left Barkingside in 1947 in the *Ormonde,* I had it with me. At Burwood it disappeared. At one of the Sunday school concerts I saw it being played on stage by my little sister and I never saw it again. I was supposed to be uncontrollable at one stage and Miss Dobbie sent me for assessment but I have had a happily married life in Australia and I love the bush setting of our home.

Cliff Remmer
1948

I was named Clifford, second child of Mable Remmer. My mother was in domestic service but did not stay long at any of her jobs. After the birth of my half sister Elizabeth in 1933 mother took a position in Thirsk, leaving Elizabeth with the maternal grandparents. When mother became pregnant with me she entered the Richmond Institution, where I was born in 1935, and stayed on working in the laundry for two years. Then as a waitress at the Bedale Hunt Hotel, she was allowed to have me there. The drunken landlord of the hotel ill-treated me. My grand parents were unwilling to take me, so in February 1938 I was placed with a foster mother a Mrs L~, who charged nine shillings a week exclusive of clothing. My case was placed on the A B O list and Dr Barnardo's payed 4 shillings a week towards my maintenance. My condition on entering foster care was of poor physical condition and terrified of strangers. Mother took a situation in Leeds, and was very regular with her payments in respect of me until she married and two months later gave birth to my other half sister June. My mother then applied for my admission as she could no longer afford to support me and she seemed to have no affection for me. I was left in foster care with Mrs L~ at Catterick until November and Dr Barnardo's payed ten shillings a week for my lodgings. I have mixed feelings about Mrs L~. According

to Barnardo's report she was an excellent foster mother and that I made rapid improvement in response to her kind treatment. I have different memories. There probably were good times in my stay there. I remember I had a blackbird that had fallen out of it's nest and I hand-reared it in the laundry. It was my only friend and it would fly out and meet me when I came home from school but one day it flew away and I never saw it again.

The beatings, probably some of them were well deserved but at no time in my life did I get punished as severely as I did by Mrs L~. The first beating I remember was one night in bed. Mrs L~ came up, (we shared the same room) and I was facing her as she got undressed, she looked over and saw I had my eyes open so she came over and gave me a thrashing saying this will stop you looking and she was right, I never looked again.

Another time I took a pound note off the dresser (I knew it was money but had no idea how much) and gave it to a boy at school for a partridge egg. The boy's father brought the pound back and I took a beating I have never forgot. After the beating she went out leaving me there crying my eyes out and feeling very sorry for myself when there was a knock on the door. I didn't open it as I had been told not to but in walked two gipsies who asked me why I was crying.

One day some people came to show us all about Australia, they showed us movies about the land of milk and honey with kids riding horses to school and picking apples off trees as they rode by. It looked wonderful to me so when they asked if anyone would like to go and live there my hand shot up like a rocket. After several trips to London for medical checks and dental work everything was ready for my big adventure

I told them and they had a good laugh and left. In 1943 I was sent to Ripon's E O D (Ever Open Door) Home and inducted into Dr Barnardo's Homes. Shortly afterwards I was moved to Eastby near Skipton Yorkshire.

177

The next home was at Annesley in the beautiful New Forest. I had never lived in a house as grand as this. It was breathtaking as you walked into the foyer with it's parquetry wood floors and blue crystal lights and the knight in shining armour standing near the coat stand. Then you walked through the door into the great dining hall and on the left a grand staircase, like in *Gone with the Wind,* and a balcony all the way round so you could look down into the dining hall. The bedrooms were on the first floor and the staff quarters were up in the roof. I must say that on the whole my stay at Annesley was a good experience.

I have had a good life in Australia. I've been happily married for 40 years with three daughters, six grand-daughters and one great grand-daughter.

Mother had a three year old and then twins, my brother and me. She had puerperal fever and post partem depression and couldn't cope. I went to Folkestone Babies Castle aged ten weeks.

Dot ~
1949

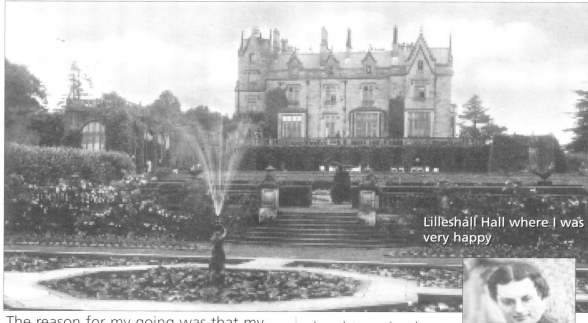

Lilleshall Hall where I was very happy

The reason for my going was that my parents and the two boys went to my grandparents three bedroomed home in Caerphilly when mother was unwell. They already had a great-uncle living with them, so there was no room for a baby as well. My grandparents always sent money to the Homes. My mother never really recovered. When I was three my father died at sea. Mother stayed on at Caerphilly. I was boarded out from the age of three to the age of ten.

When war broke out, I was evacuated to a Barnardo's Home in Shropshire where the woman in charge, a Bishop's

daughter, simply didn't like children, a martinet who made

Miss Elizabeth Job

little rules all the time and wanted to be addressed as Madame. I spoke up for another girl after she received what we used to call a public belting, and threatened to report her to the authorities at Stepney. After the one teacher I liked left, I watched her disappearing down the road and ran away five miles to another home, Lilleshall. This was a gracious stately home, belonging to the Duke and Duchess of Sutherland. I knew where it was because I had been there on guide outings. A Miss Job was in charge. I said breathlessly that I had run away and was never going back and she laughed and said to come and tell her all about it.

178

Miss Job suggested to me when I was 18 that I would have a better chance in Australia and she asked Barnardo's in Sydney to sponsor me out. I was 20 when I came out in the *Asturias*.

Miss Job was a huge influence in my life. I was a naughty girl and I don't know what would have happened to me without her loving influence. She changed my life. She became my mentor and later encouraged me to come out to Australia and to take up nursing. I did this and nursed until my retirement.

I found out later from her unmarried sister that she had escaped the Nazis in France in 1941 by helping to row an open boat across the Channel with six Jewish girls that she had been teaching. She took the girls to Barnardo's and they were so impressed with her heroic act and her devotion to children, they offered her the position of Superintendent at Lilleshall. She stayed there until it closed in 1945, then went to Broughton Hall, Chester, which was for little boys then retired to Bournemouth. Miss Job was Welsh and formed a choir of about 40 girls and we used to give local performances of English folk songs. I was so lucky to meet her. I loved her dearly and we regularly corresponded until the day she died.

I kept in touch with my family. After my grandfather had died, grandmother(Nain in Welsh), became very dour. 'Promise me you'll never marry an Englishman!', she

Ward sister in charge at Newcastle Hospital about 1960

used to say. She was happy that I married an Australian, because he wasn't English! She said, 'that's fine, dear, he's a colonial!'She said I wouldn't inherit her property if I went to Australia and I didn't! Her local hospital benefitted by my migration!

179

Asturias

Postwar children were prized by both the United Kingdom and Australia after the horrific death toll from the war. They were seen as the future of the country rather than as surplus to the country's needs or as labour. Australia pressed the London authorities for more and more children.

Director, Child Welfare Department to the Department of Immigration regarding the adoption of children from the UK: 'the arrangements in this respect do not appear satisfactory...'

From Australia House, London, To Arthur Calwell, Minister for Immigration: 'the whole problem of child immigration rests, not either with the people at home or with us here in London, but is entirely one where the individual organisation seems to have fallen down'.

' a desperate position exists in the UK regarding the tonsil operations not being performed because of the presence of infantile paralysis in epidemic form...a proportion of children have signs of old rickets.

Noel Lamidey Chief Migration Officer: 'It is a fair statement to make that throughout the whole of the child migration nominations we have passed the initiative in all cases to the organisations. We have prompted them, given them application forms, and kept them constantly under review ...there is no further advice we can take to get the children'.

18/2/48 SMH By cable: ' The governors of Dr Barnardo's decided yesterday to register orphans under the *Adoption of Children Act*, which will permit some of the children in the care of Homes to be adopted by private families. The governors had resisted this step for many years. They act mainly because of present difficulties in housing the Home's 7 000 children.

To The Hon Arthur Calwell from W B Ladd, Manager NSW: 'I am very concerned that the 'male escort for 20 boys and 3 older boys and girls should very definitely be 'one of our people''

The Fifties, the End of Child Migration and the Future

AUSTRALIA

ENGLAND

Shirley Ronge
1950

Little Bardfield Hall, a Tudor mansion loaned to Barnardo's during the war. Everybody was very happy there. Our popular Matron Kitty Edwards was the subject of a This Is Your Life programme on TV

Matron Kitty above with five of the 60 evacuees, ranging from two weeks old babies to ten year olds, which she cared for while WWII was raging. She managed Bardfield, which had a farm attached and a staff of 30 and was loved by all for her fairness and loving ways

I was put into Barnardos when I was four years old because according to the authorities my mother was no longer able to look after me.

The Maloja

My mother was made pregnant by her employer, like so many girls of that time. She lived and worked on his estate with her parents in the west of England. My mother later had a second illegitimate child, whom she kept, with a serviceman during the war. She eventually married a widower with three children. He promised her that she could bring me home if she married him but never fulfilled that promise. She subsequently had one more child.

I lived in seven different Homes. Whilst in the Midlands, when I was 11 years old, I was asked if I would like to go to Australia. As I had been learning about it at school, I said yes. My mother took 18 months to consent which she said she would only do if she heard from my lips that I wanted to go. I was taken to see her at a Home in Plymouth. She was bawling her eyes out. She had a six year old girl with her and a baby by her new husband. I was old enough to realise that her position was hopeless. From the day I arrived I can honestly say all I wanted was to go home to England.

In 1979 I finally managed it. My mother had been mentally and physically abused by her husband over a long period. He had also intercepted many letters we had written to each other. Many were found unopened after her death. I needed to talk with her on my own, so my brother took my stepfather out for a day and my mum and I sat and talked and wept profusely.

I found my mother very nervous and in a bad state of health. Although we were so happy to be together, it was a critical time for her, as she told me her whole difficult life story. It was utterly impossible to help in a two week stay and I promised to return. But my journey of 12 000 miles and the unresolved issues from the past that it stirred up I feel contributed to her taking her life two days after I left.

I used to put a photo of my friend's father up and look at it and think what a marvellous thing it would be to have one...

Maurice Priest 1950

On admittance to Barnardo's aged two years

Aged 15 before leaving for Australia

Tall Ships by Maurice Priest

184

I was born in 1932 at Hull, one of four children all named after film stars. I was named after Maurice Chevalier. My father was a railway signals fitter's labourer. My parents had separated and my father tried to kill himself although in 1942 he was in the RAF and wrote to me. In 1939, mum wrote, sending one shilling. I was evacuated to Creeke Abbey, Fakenham, Norfolk in 1938. We slept on the floor until we found some beds. We had a lot of fun, always up to mischief with the local farmers often after us for scrumping apples and moving their machinery about.

By 1945 I was in Watts Naval Training School, aged 14, and I used to play the bugle, last post, lights out. Boys at Watts were known by their numbers, like mine was 120, which I had to play

on the bugle. We wore short pants in all weathers. At Watts, if the boys ran away, when they returned nobody was allowed to talk to them for a week or two. The bad boys copped the cane a lot. I only got it a few times.

A certain height was needed for the Navy and I left and got lodgings and some work in a nursery. One of the lodgers suggested I apply for Australia.

Barnardo's was good to us. They protected you. I've seen kids brought up in private homes and they haven't had what we've had. I've had a long happy marriage. My wife always wanted me to trace my past. She was left some money and we went to the UK in 1985. I now have a photo of my father.

I came out in 1950. There were 25 boys and nine girls. In 1949, we were asked if we wanted to go to Australia. I remember they showed us a bush burning, like the one in the biblical story and told us it was a bush fire!

Michael Oldfield
1950

When I said I'd like to go to Australia, they told me I had a twin sister. 'Have I?' I asked in surprise. We had been evacuated together, (I remember one of our Spitfires crashing at the back of a beautiful house belonging to the Duke of Norfolk and used by Barnardo's, where we lived), but I had become sick and been sent back to Foley House. I had a great time at Foley. The Superintendent and his wife treated us all like family. They couldn't do enough for us. For two years I was Best Boy of the Year. Tom Price encouraged me to learn the piano and gave me a love of classical music.

We were born at St Pancras Hospital and my father, who never married my mother, was killed in action in France. Mother worked at a big house. She was advised by her employer to put us in a home when we were four years old.

My sister came out in November 1947, in the first party after the war. When the ship I was on docked, she was brought down and introduced to me by the manager at Barnardo's. I wouldn't have recognised her in the crowds. Then I went to Mowbray Park and she went back to Burwood.

Mother became a distant memory as I went to work in Gulgong, for really good employers, Eric and Norma, and then as chef at Prince Alfred Hospital. I'm still working there.

My sister became a model and then a successful businesswoman and now lives in America.

I wanted to find my mother and Tom Price let me look at my file. This became my map to return to the village where I was born and find my people. In 1980 I hired a car and drove to the Fitzwilliam Arms in Peterborough. My father had been a thatcher for the Earl of Fitzwilliam for years. I managed to find my mother's phone number through the local post office and rang her. I told her very carefully not to be shocked and to sit down but that I was her son returned from Australia.

She asked me to give her some time, but I was greeted with open arms straight away by some aunties that I found. I finally met my mother in the Victoria Hotel in London in 1984, when she was in her eighties. I took her out for dinner.

185

I feel no bitterness that I was put into Barnardo's by my mother. My life has been one of great joy, both personally and in public life, and that is my greatest benefit.

Gordon Lewis 1950

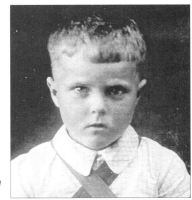

Aged two. I realised recently that I had a black eye on admission

A very pleasant duty - conducting a naturalisation ceremony while Acting Mayor of Wingecarribee Shire Council

I was born out of wedlock in 1932. My new stepfather refused responsibility for me and I was boarded out at six months. When I was three and a half, the wagon rolled up to the door with a row of children sitting either side and one at the back, and I was put in.

I was fostered out at eight years and had to carry bags of coal on my back to earn a shilling. I am now a councillor and have been Deputy Mayor in the Southern Highlands. After 60 years through the local parish church, I went back and found my mother, aged 84 years and still very active, and my half-brother and half-sister. My mother had made a pact never to speak of me and it was a great surprise to my new found

family.

Because of my love of soccer, I've had a long and happy association with soccer organisations, some of which have honoured me with life membership.

I came out in the *Asturias*. My greatest personal achievement is that of my marriage to Bette, our two sons and their wives and grandchildren.

The Georgic came out in 1955

The Asturias came out in October 1950

Parties arriving by ship in the fifties:

1950 *Maloja Asturias*
1951 *Ormonde*
1952 *Strathmere*
1953 *Chitral New Australia*
1954 *Otranto*
1955 *Iberia Georgic*
1956 *Orontes Otranto*
1957 no parties arrived
1958 *Fairsea*
1959 *Strathnaver Fairsea*

Hilda Fudge
1951

In this photograph of my ancestors, the man in military uniform was deceased when this was taken. They must have grouped themselves around his photograph

Tom Price and his wife Joy, (Pop and Auntie Joy), brought us out in 1951 in the *Ormonde*. My mother had died in January 1948 at our home in Poole, Dorset. The family fell apart as my father, an Army man, knew nothing about bringing up children. My older sister and brother had already left home to go out to work. With four children left at home, I wasn't quite nine and the youngest was only ten months old. My cousin adopted the baby. Father remarried shortly afterwards and I ran away to stay with my grandma.

I was sent to a council home a couple of years later when gran became too old to look after me. In June 1951, I came home from Guides and a man in a suit asked if I wanted to go to Australia with Dorothy and Fred where we could ride ponies to school! I went to High Broome, Crowborough for three months and then to Barkingside for medical examinations. I met Dorothy and Fred there and we came out together. We were parted for a short time and were reunited at Greenwood.

I knew my family and I was always able to catch up with them and build on relationships. We were very happy at Greenwood. We loved being there.

We loved to feed and ride the pony at Greenwood

l to r Dorothy, Fred and Hilda at the 1992 Picton Re-union.

Our 'Pop' was determined that his girls were not going into domestic service. Looking back I realise how lucky we were to have him. I went to work at South British Insurance Company as a shorthand typist. Dorothy, my sister, went to David Jones and Fred went to Picton and then the country and loved it.

Dorothy now lives in Kingaroy, Queensland. She is mother to two girls and a boy. One son died aged 11 in a car accident. She is Nana to 11 grand-children.

Fred lives in Lithgow, NSW and has three step-children and is Poppy to four grand-children. Emma and Monique absolutely adore him. I have one son and am Nana to Peter Thomas. Another grand-child is due in February 2000.

I have been very fortunate to have made two trips 'home', to find family - aunts, uncles, cousins. They were very surprised that after such a long time I could remember them and where they all lived. My first trip was in 1976, my second in 1990, when I found a lot of the older ones had passed away. I still have a brother and a sister in the UK.

While searching out the relatives, I came up with a French horn player in Sir Daniel Godfreys Band, Joe Di Marion and a film actor from the 40s, Alan Fudge.

189

I wrote a book about my life, *Dr Barnardo's Homes and Me* in 1988. The following is an extract:

June Reid
1952

June in the front, 1949. Many Barnardo's children had never seen the sea

Me on the left aged eight and a half at Beehive Cottage, Barkingside.

190

It was the 27th November 1946, I was sitting on a long wooden bench with my little sister Anne beside me. We were both swinging our skinny little legs together. Anne copied everything I did! She was sitting next to our mother....

This was the day my mother was putting me into Dr Barnardo's Homes. The bench we were sitting on was at the Boys Garden City, Woodford Bridge, Essex. We saw a door open. A lady stepped out of a room and called my name out. I got off the bench slowly. Anne quickly grabbed my left hand to come with me. My mother caught hold of Anne in time to stop her, told her 'No Anne! Just June this time'.

I remember the woman started to fit me up with new clothes. I thought this was terrific. I even asked if Anne was going to get new clothes too.

I wanted to go out to the big hall where we were all waiting before to show my new clothes to Anne and my mother. Before anyone could stop me...I was standing where my mother and sister had been but they were not there anymore, they had all gone ...and didn't even say goodbye to me.

On the lawn at Burwood

Tom Price
'Pop'

Tom Price, affectionately known as 'Pop' by many of his charges, was born in a gamekeeper's lodge on the estate of the Duke of Westminster's Home in Cheshire. He was only nine years old when his father died and he helped his mother with the other children. He joined the Royal Navy in 1935 and concluded service as Senior Lieutenant. Disabled out of the Royal Navy after contracting viral meningitis when on active service, Tom saw distinguished service from Dunkirk to D Day. He was on the Russian convoys and served under Lord Louis Mountbatten. His love of the naval life led him to Watts Naval Training School for boys from Barnardo. With his wife, he managed a home in Eastbourne, Sussex, caring for about 80 charges for three years before emigrating.

Tom migrated with 40 boys and girls in 1951 to open Greenwood at Normanhurst, the first home for boys and girls together.

Tom Price worked to provide small homes or family units rather than institutional establishments. As well as Scone, homes were set up at Canberra, Belmont, Ryde, Kiama, Wollongong, Lindfield, Cronulla and Wahroonga and he was responsible for the first Child Care Complex at Auburn.

The last party of children was brought out by Tom's wife and daughter Heather in 1964 in the *Oriana*. Tom was invested with an MBE and retired from Barnardo's in 1976.

191

Paul Schmitt
1958

The authorities put me in Barkingside, where I was happy and felt secure among all the other children, although I had part of my hand missing and a German sounding surname, (not forgetting this was just after the war!).

I was fostered out aged seven to a spinster, kind and loving. My mother continually interfered. Father had been in the French Army. He returned and my mother made a big effort to have me and my brother reunited with them. I was ten years old at the time. I found out years later that my younger brother had been put in a different home.

They took us off to Luxembourg, where my sister was born soon after we arrived, but neither of my parents understood what parenting was about and it wasn't long before I was sent back to England and Barnardo's.

192

I arrived in Australia in January 1958 and was taken to Mowbray Park, where I stayed for about 18 months and finished my schooling at Picton High. I left just on 15.

From there I worked on a variety of farms, tobacco, fruit and cattle and anything that I could turn my hand at and learn from, all over New South Wales and Queensland, trying to find my niche in life. I eventually married my best friend and we have two sons, and are still together after 35 years.

After a few more jobs I ended up in the coal mines in the Burragorang Valley which I thoroughly enjoyed. Unfortunately, had an accident that made me unfit to work, not a happy prospect. I was only 33. When our sons finished their education, we retired to the north coast of NSW, where we have lived for about 12 years. I fill in much of my time painting, which I've always enjoyed. Unfortunately this was not a talent that could be fostered at Barnardo's, in those days. You were looked on as being a bit odd. People seem to enjoy my landscapes . My favourite painters would be Norman Lindsay, then Leonard Long.

The Peak by Paul Schmitt

I was put into the care of Dr Barnardo's in 1948, as far as I know, as my mother was not really capable of looking after children. This was after falling on a live railway line and being electrocuted so severely that I lost part of my right hand, which was to affect me for the rest of my life. I was three and a half at the time and out on my own.

Me on coming out to Australia

The Painter by Paul Schmitt

The Stagecoach by Paul Schmitt

193

When Margaret and Paul moved up to the north coast, they began organising reunions for Barnardo people unable to get to the annual gathering at Picton. They became annual events. Margaret and Paul are often visited by old boys or girls travelling through as well as those living locally. They telephone or write, sharing family news and visit them in their homes. Everyone seems to enjoy themselves and the opportunity to talk and reminisce about their early lives.

I was born in Leicester in 1946. When I was nine years old my father died in an industrial accident. I was one of nine children and my mother was unable to cope so I was placed into a Dr Barnardo's home in Eastbourne, Sussex.

Michael Bayes
1959

We now have four beautiful, successful children. Julie owns a fashion boutique and I am employed by a large meat processors as a human resource manager.

The Bayes family at Parkdale, Parkville in 1998 at Christopher's wedding. (l back) Jonathan Patricia Michael Julie Michelle (f)Christopher and Fiona

194

I felt very sad because I was not allowed outside the home, except to go to school, and I never saw any of my family again. When I was 12 years old they asked me if I wanted to go to Australia and I said yes because I thought I would enjoy spending six weeks on a boat and having a new adventure.

Upon arrival I went to a new home at Belmont NSW under the care of Ralph and Dorothy Green. This was a new family type home of around 15 people and much better than the institutional type homes in England where there were large numbers of boys with very strict rules. When I was aged 14, I left school and went to the Barnardo's Training Farm at Tooloogan Vale, Scone. The Manager was Andrew Crawford

who was an inspiration to all of the boys and had a major impact in making some of these days the most enjoyable and memorable of my life in Barnardo's.

I enjoyed the bush life, working on several properties in the Scone district. I eventually bought my own small farm and together with my wife Julie set about restoring the federation homestead.

During 1944 I was fortunate enough to return to the UK in search of my family. Unable to locate my mother, I did stay with my brother who ironically owns a pub in Eastbourne called *The Dinkum*. After 36 years this was a very happy occasion for me. I am still in regular contact with him.

During the fifties, child migration was arranged by: Dr Barnardo's Homes, The Fairbridge Society, Northcote Children's Emigration Fund for Australia, The National Children's Home and Orphanage, The Church of England Advisory Council of Empire Settlement, The Church of Engand's Children's Society and The Catholic Council for British Overseas Settlement.

The End of Child Migration

On arrival, institutions approved for the reception of child migrants in New South Wales were: The Big Brother Movement at Liverpool and Homebush, the Fairbridge Farm School at Molong, Dr Barnardo's Homes, consisting of the Farm School at Picton, the Girls Home at Burwood, Greenwood for Boys and Girls at Normanhurst: The Methodist Home for Children, Dalmar at Carlingford, the Church of England Boys and Girls Home at Carlingford and the United Protestant Association Home, Melrose at Parramatta.

There were five Roman Catholic orphanages at Thurgoona, Mayfield, Lane Cove, West Maitland and Ryde and St Vincent's Boys' Home at Parramatta. The Big Brother Movement at Liverpool and Picton Farm had the majority of child migrants by far.

In pace with changing perspectives in society, the whole idea of child migration became unacceptable. The reasons why will be explored fully in *After Barnardo 2*. Parties arrived by sea in the *Strathnaver* in 1959, the *Orontes* in 1960, the *Stratheden* in 1961, the *Oriana* in 1962, the *Fairsky* in 1963, and the *Oriana* in 1964. The last Barnardo Party of seven boys arrived in April 1965 by air.

195

The 1956 Party

The Future

In the last few hectic weeks of publication, I received a postcard of the Bridge of Sighs at Cambridge from Myfanwy, whose story is on page 57.

Dear Ann, Thought you might be interested to know I've been to Wales and met many of my cousins and two remaining aunts on my mother's side. I'm still trying to trace my father's side of the family...this seems difficult, but I am in touch with TRACELINE, who will do a search. If they can't help I'll try another group...'

In their response to the Select Health Committee Report on Child Migrants, A Travel (Support) Fund has been proposed by the British Government, raising immediate concerns. It is evident from the accounts in this book that children should never be taken from their family group except in the most extreme circumstances as when the good doctor saved children's lives. Myfanwy, now retired, is one of so many searching for their broken roots, trying to still the haunting questions. A financial gesture from a government many years after the event cannot heal their pasts and in many cases opens a Pandora's box of further rejection, disruption of their present existence and inability to retain relationships from the other side of the world. Young Maurice Priest, used to prop up a photograph of someone else's father and think how wonderful it would be to have one. The power of blood ties must be acknowledged by society to be crucial .

Migrant children were haplessly caught up in social tensions with their parents and often there was no choice for them.

Today with genetic engineering, everyone has multiple choice: whether to become pregnant, to continue with the pregnancy, to choose the gender, when to give birth, and whether to remain with the other parent. Over-riding this is genetic manipulation where a single child can have four parents: the donor, surrogate mother, the parents, (who may be of the same gender). This implies eight grandparents and a wide community of interested relations.

Establishment practice and law is, as in the time of Dr Barnardo, lagging sadly behind these practices. A genetically engineered child not informed of its biological parent could meet a sibling and feel attracted to them, not knowing that they are related.

In dealing with the intricacies of human behaviour and the leaps of progress made by science, one still small voice should prevail: babies are people at a different stage of growth and powerless to defend themselves for many years. They must be nurtured, informed and given their past.

For the past fourteen years, in response to changing perceptions in society, Barnardos has made a new approach to helping the most vulnerable children in our society accept their past and come to terms with their present situation. Old girls and boys experiences and suggestions have been utilised in preparing a 'life story book' on an individual basis. A counsellor goes through the book with the child, who freely asks questions and makes suggestions. It might only contain fragments, but it can have detailed information which they can continually add to, depending on the situation. It will give them strength to face the future.

Louise Voigt
CEO Barnardo Australia

The good Doctor diplomatically leaving the Royal Presence at a concert - children never behave well when it is imperative!

The *UN Convention on the Rights of the Child.* Ratified by 20 countries, the Convention became international law in 1990. There is no judicial machinery to enforce the law and no right of individual compensation. In the preamble it states in part:
'...recognising that the child, for the full and harmonious development of his or her personality, shall grow up in a family environment, in an atmosphere of happiness, love and understanding...'

Under 'identity', Article 8 states:
Parties undertake to respect the right of the child to preserve his or her identity, including nationality, name and family relations, as recognised by law, without unlawful interference.

Books

Appleyard, R.T., *British Emigration to Australia*, (Australia,1964).

Barnardo, Mrs. and Marchant, J. *Barnardo*, (UK,

Best, G., *Memoirs of the late Dr Barnardo, Mid-Victorian Britain*,(UK,1979)

Bean, P and Melville, J. *Lost Children of the Empire*, (UK,1989)

Borrie, W.D., *European Peopling of Australasia, A demographic history*, 1788-88, (Australia,1994).

Bowlby J., *Childcare and the Growth of Love*, (UK,1953).

Edelman H., *Motherless Daughters*, (Australia,1994).

Fabian, S. and M., *Children in Australia: an outline history*, (Australia, 1980).

Fairbridge, K., *The Autobiography of Kingsley Fairbridge*, (UK,1928).

Furman E.,*Child's Parent Dies,* (A), (USA,1974).

Childhood Memories, Barnardos, (UK,1995).

Gill, A., *Orphans of the Empire:*, (Australia,1997).

Himmelfarb,G.,*Victorian Minds A Study of Intellectuals in Crisis and Ideologies in Transition*, (USA,1968).

Humphries, S.G. and P., *Labour of Love: the Experience of Parenthood in Britain*,1900-1950, (UK,1993).

Humphreys, M., *Empty Cradles*, (UK,1994 1st edit).

Lane, J., *Fairbridge Kid,* (Australia,1990).

MacRobertson, *MacRobertson Abroad*, (UK,1927).

Miles R.,*Children We Deserve, (The)*, (UK,1995).

Moore, A, *Growing Up with Barnardos,*(Australia,1990).

Macintyre, S., *Succeeding Age,(The)*,The Oxford History of Australia Vol.4, (Australia, 1987).

Owen, D., *English Philanthropy,1660-1960*, (UK,1965).

Palmer, G.,*Reluctant Refugee*, (Australia,1998).

Parr, J., *Labouring Children*, (Croom Helm,1980).

Roe, M., *Australia, Britain and Migration 1915-1940: a study of desperate hopes*, Australia,1995).

Rose, J., *For the Sake of the Children*, (Australia,1987).

Sherrington, G., *Australia's immigrants 1788-1978*, (Australia).

Titmuss, Richard and Kay, *A Man and Wife*: (UK,1996).

Wagner G., *Barnardo,* (UK,1979).

Wagner G., *Children of the Empire,* (UK,1982).

Documents/Periodicals

Study of the history of welfare work in Sydney from 1788 till about 1900, D.Peyser, JRAHS,25(3), part 2, pp169-212.

MILLIONS MAGAZINE, May 1, 1920 to February 15, 1922.

B. Coldrey, *Child migrants in Post war Britain*, HISTORY, September 1997, pp 20-23

Coldrey, B.M., *Child Migration and the Catholic Church*, JRAHS, (3/4), Australia 1993, pp 199-213.

Dr Barnardos: *Building of Ideal Homes - Migration,* Illustrated Monthly, 18 p16 Sydney 1923 325.342 D

Peyser, D., *A study of the history of welfare work in Sydney, from 1788 till about 1900,* JRAHS, 25 (3),169-212, Part2.

British Youth and Empire settlement - the Dreadnought boys in NSW, JRAHS, 82(1), pp1-22.

Documents/Periodicals-continued

Annual Reports, 32-33, Dr Barnardos Homes
Annual Reports in Aus Mitchell Library call no:Q 362.799094/3.
Annual Report, Dr Barnardo's Homes in Australia, 1889, 208/p27.
Annual Report, Dr Barnardo's Homes, Australia Branch, 1926/62.
Annual Report, Dr Barnardo's Homes, London, 1889, no.67-68, 1932-3.
Health and Physical Culture, December 1st, 1938.
Help (Sydney, Australia, undated).
SMH, March 1891
Sun Herald, *Don't abandon us Di pleas from Dr B's.* 21 7 96 p.30
Sunday Times:27/6/93 *How Britain sent its Children into Exile*
The Times:*Barnardo's leave for Australia,* Aug 27 11d Aug 4 10e 1921
The Times :1906 23 2 11b

Archival Collections
Barnardo Publications

Barnardos Guild Messenger, The, Winter 1997,(UK 1997).

Newspapers

The Times 1877-1987
The Sydney Morning Herald

Official Publications and Reports
United Kingdom

Custody of Children Act, 1891 (Barnardo Act).
Children and Young Persons Act,1933.
Children Act, 1948.
Children Act, 1958.
Children and Young Persons Act, 1963.
Children and Young Persons Act, 1969.
Children Act 1975.
Child Care Act, 1980.
Foster Children Act, 1980.

Australia

Connecting Kin - Guide to Records, 1998 Dept of Community Services NSW.

A NUMBER OF AGENCIES HOLD RECORDS AND OFFER SUPPORT AND
COUNSELLING SERVICES. THESE INCLUDE:
BARNARDO'S ADOPTION AGENCY
Australia contact phone number: (02) 9281 5510
United Kingdom contact ph. no: 0011 44 181 550 882